Oscar Israelowitz's

The Jewish Heritage Trail of New York

Note: This publication is not affiliated with "Heritage Trails New York" nor the
Museum of Jewish Heritage–A Living Memorial to the Holocaust

Israelowitz Publishing
P.O.Box 228   Brooklyn, NY 11229
Tel. (718) 951-7072

Library of Congress Catalog Number: 98-71749
International Standard Book Number: 1-878741-37-3

Printed in the U. S. A. By:

Moriah Offset Corp.

115 Empire Blvd. Brooklyn, N.Y. 11225, Tel: (718) 693-3800

Contents

5   Financial District

43   Chinatown

45   Lower East Side

87   East Village

93   Greenwich Village

99   Midtown West

105 Upper West Side

115 Midtown East

120 Upper East Side

131 Places of Interest

159 Eating Kosher

163 Where to Pray

167 Biography

168 Catalog

170 Tours

173 Index

Financial

District

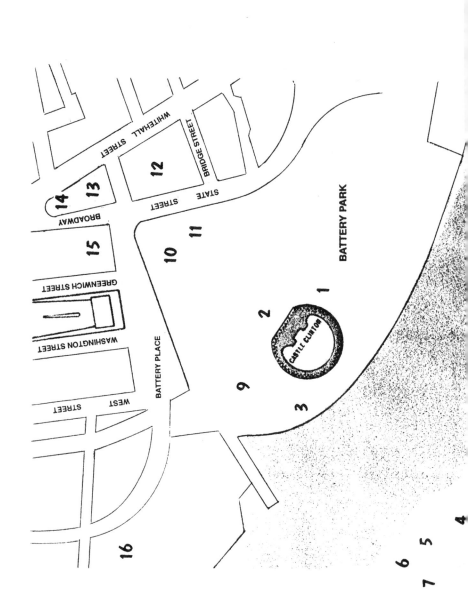

BROADWAY

WHITEHALL STREET

BRIDGE STREET

STATE STREET

12

13

14

15

16

GREENWICH STREET

WASHINGTON STREET

BATTERY PLACE

WEST STREET

10

11

9

2

1

3

CASTLE CLINTON

BATTERY PARK

6

7

5

4

STOP 1.

CASTLE CLINTON NATIONAL MONUMENT

Castle Clinton is a product of the Napoleonic era. The conflict between France and Great Britain plus the English policy of seizing American ships and impressing American seamen into the British Navy produced this tension. The climax came on June 22, 1807, with the British attack upon the American frigate Chesapeake. In New York, mass meetings denounced the attack. At the same time, a great "fortification fever" swept the city, for New York, except for Fort Columbus on Governors Island, was virtually defenseless.

In short order, five new forts were built; Fort Wood on Bedloes Island, Fort Gibson on Ellis Island, three-tiered Castle Williams on Governors Island, the South-west Battery at the tip of Manhattan Island, and the North Battery at the foot of Hubert Street.

Circular in shape, the South-west Battery stood in about 35 feet of water, 200 feet from shore. A timber causeway with drawbridge connected the new fort to Manhattan. The South-west Battery had 28 guns on one tier. Inside the rounded ends of the rear wall, on the land side, were the magazines. Quarters for the officers were at each side of the passageway to the causeway. There were no barracks for the enlisted men.

The South-west Battery was completed in 1811. Throughout the War of 1812 the fort stood ready, but its guns fired at nothing more dangerous than a harmless hulk moored in the river for target practice. At the end of the war, the fort was named Castle Clinton in honor of DeWitt Clinton, a former mayor of New York City and later governor of New York State. In 1823, Castle Clinton was ceded to New York City. The following year it was leased by the city as a place of public entertainment.

Opened as Castle Garden on July 3, 1824, it soon became one of the favored "places of resort" in New York. The interior was described as a "fanciful garden, tastefully ornamented with shrubs and flowers." In time, a great fountain was installed. The Garden was the setting for band concerts, fireworks, an occasional balloon ascension, and demonstrations of the latest scientific achievements. The gunrooms, decorated with marble busts and painted panoramas, became a promenade. The officers' quarters became a bar selling choice liquors, confections and ice.

In the 1840s, Castle Garden was roofed over and more serious entertainment was added to the fare. The Garden then presented operas, in concert form. On September 11, 1850, P.T. Barnum presented the Swedish Nightingale, Jenny Lind, in her American debut. More than six thousand people filled Castle Garden for that concert.

On August 3, 1855, Castle Garden, under lease to the State of New York, was opened as an immigrant landing depot. Between 1855 and 1889, more than eight million immigrants–two out of every three persons immigrating to the United States in this period–passed through the Garden. Castle Garden was closed as an immigration depot on April 18,

1890 because of corruption and political scandals. Has anything changed in New York City in one hundred years?

The Yiddish term Kessel Garten refers to this original immigration depot, Castle Garden. It refers to a chaotic scene of hundreds of immigrants not knowing what to do or where to go. The term carried-over to the Ellis Island Immigration Depot , where things seemed to be just as chaotic. The term was actually used in every immigration depot in the United States, whether it was in Boston, Baltimore or Galveston, Texas.

In 1896, Castle Clinton was once again altered, this time to become the New York Aquarium. The Aquarium was moved to Coney Island in 1941.

Today, Castle Clinton has been restored to its original 1811 fortress design. It is a National Historic Monument and is administered by the National Park Service. Be sure to go inside the small museum which features 3D scale models of the development of Lower Manhattan, from the early 1800s to the twentieth century. The museum is located just to the right of the massive wooden and iron doors (if you are coming from Battery Park and down the steps). On some Sundays, some of the Park Rangers dress in full 18th century military costume, complete with muskets. There are daily tours of the facilities given by the Park Rangers at noon.

Tickets to the Statue of Liberty and Ellis Island ferry can be purchased at the kiosk in the center of Castle Clinton. For ferry information call (212) 269-5755.

Walk out the double massive doors of Castle Clinton, look north, toward the huge skyscrapers. Go up the stairs and you will see...

Stop 2.

MONUMENT TO THE IMMIGRANTS

This mass of humanity symbolizes the millions of immigrants who struggled to leave their impoverished homelands in search for freedom and tolerance. Some of the figures in the lower foreground appear to have yarmulkas (Jewish head coverings) on their heads.

If you turn left at the top of the stairs, walk along the perimeter of Castle Clinton and when you get to the open promenade, turn right. Look for a raised platform (about three feet high) surrounded by hedges. You are at...

Stop 3.

EMMA LAZARUS PLAQUE

Immigrants arriving on Ellis Island.
Photo Credit: Lewis Hine
International Museum of Photography: George Eastman House

If you don't have a chance to go out to the base of the Statue of Liberty, a copy of Emma Lazarus' historic sonnet, *The New Colossus*, has been copied on a copper plaque. It is embedded in Jerusalem limestone. Emma Lazarus was a descendent of the first Sephardic Jewish community which arrived in New Amsterdam in September, 1654. The key phrase of her sonnet is *Give me your tired, your poor, your huddled masses yearning to breathe free.*

Turn around and look out at the harbor. You will see four interesting sights, starting with the Statue of Liberty...

Stop 4.
STATUE OF LIBERTY

The Statue of Liberty is the monument and symbol of freedom and hope for millions of immigrants. The statue was constructed in 1876 and presented by France to the United States as a gift in honor of its Centennial anniversary. The statue was fabricated from 100 tons of copper hammered out to a thickness of 3/32nds of an inch and spread over 125 tons of steel. It was shipped across the Atlanic Ocean in 214 crates. It took an additional ten years to complete the pedestal upon which the statue stands. The pedestal was designed by Richard Morris Hunt. The dedication was in October, 1886.
The Statue of Liberty was designed by Frederik Bartholdi and engineered by Gustav Eifel, the designer of the Eifel Tower in Paris. At the base of the statue is a plaque bearing the sonnet, *The New Colossus*, by Emma Lazarus. The sonnet is recognized by its key phrase, *Give me your tired, your poor, your huddled masses yearning to breathe free.*

Look to the right of the Statue of Liberty, at the cluster of old red brick buildings. The largest of those buildings (with its large water towers) is the Ellis Island Immigration Museum.

Stop 5.
ELLIS ISLAND IMMIGRATION MUSEUM

Ellis Island served as one of the nation's largest immigration processing centers. It was opened in 1892, following the corruption, scandals and ultimate closure of the Castle Garden Immigration Depot. During its active years as an immigration depot, over twelve million immigrants were processed on Ellis Island. The Main Arrivals Building has been restored as a museum. You can see the original Baggage Room, dormitory facilities, permanent exhibition with artifacts brought from the "Old

1875 artist's rendering of Statue of Liberty, facing the Atlanic Ocean and placed on a much taller pedestal.
Courtesy John Grafton's New York in the 19th Century (Dover)

Countries," and a wonderful film about the immigrants' journeys from Europe to the *Goldena Medina*–the United States, where is was said that the streets were paved with gold. Ellis Island can be reached only by ferry. Tickets can be purchased inside Castle Clinton (Stop 1) in Manhattan or in Liberty State Park, in Jersey City, New Jersey. Ferry tickets are $7 for adults and $3 for children under 17. For ferry schedules call (212) 269-5755.

Look to the right of Ellis Island at that magnificenet French chateau...

Stop 6.

CENTRAL RAILROAD OF NEW JERSEY TERMINAL

From1892 through 1954, the Central Railroad of New Jersey (CRRNJ) Terminal stood with the Statue of Liberty and Ellis Island to unfold one of this nation's most dramatic stories: The immigration of Northern, Southern and Eastern Europeans into the United States. After being greeted by the Statue of Liberty and processed at Ellis Island, two thirds of the 12 million immigrants boarded trains that took them to their new homes throughout the United States from this terminal.

The CRRNJ Terminal was constructed in 1889 in the French Renaissance style. In 1914, as many as 28,000 people passed through the terminal daily. The main terminal has recently been restored. It is located in Liberty State Park, Jersey City, New Jersey. It can be reached from Manhattan via the ferry to Statue of Liberty. Change on Liberty Island for the New Jersey ferry. But if you wish to return the same way, there is an additional fare. You can take the PATH Tubes from the World Trade Center to Exchange Place, and then a shuttle bus.

Just behind the CRRNJ Terminal is a complex of space-age buildings. Those are...

Stop 7.

LIBERTY SCIENCE CENTER

Located in Liberty State Park, the Liberty Science Center is a hands-on "where science=fun" interactive exhibition hall. Families can spend an entire day with hundreds of interactive exhibits on four exhibit floors. Hold a live starfish or giant exotic insect, crawl in the 100-foot-long *Touch Tunnel,* play virtual reality basketball, experience a 3D laser show, or be part of the Kodak OMNI THEATER, with the largest IMAX Dome screen in the United States. For more information call (201) 200-1000.

Stop 8.

LIBERATION MONUMENT

The Liberation Monument was designed by the noted sculptor, Nathan Rapaport. The 30-foot-high bronze monument portrays an American soldier liberating and carrying a concentration camp victim. The victim's arm is tattooed with the concentration camp number. The monument's location, just behind the Statue of Liberty and Ellis Island Immigration Museum and Manhattan's glorious skyline, makes this one of the most moving memorials to the Holocaust in the world!

To get to the Liberation Monument, take the New Jersey Turnpike to Exit 14B. Proceed down the hill, go straight, past the line of flags and beyond the Visitor's Center.

Back in Battery Park...
From the top of the stairs at Castle Clinton, take the walkway bearing left. Just behind the benches are several pine trees. You are at...

Stop 9.

JERUSALEM GROVE

In honor of the United States' Bicentennial in 1976, the mayor of Jerusalem, Teddy Kollek, presented the City of New York and then Mayor Abraham Beame, with fifteen Atlas cedars. There is a stone marker lying on the grass, about ten feet from the benches signifying this event. The stone marker is Jerusalem limestone. All buildings in the City of Jerusalem are required to be built or faced with this white stone.

From that first starting point, on the top of the stairs at Castle Clinton, walk straight ahead. This promenade lined with beautiful rose bushes, is called Emma Lazarus Walk. It used to be the wooden bridge which con - nected Manhattan to the island in the harbor which housed Castle Clinton. All of Battery Park is landfill. Continue to the flagpole and...

Stop 10.

HISTORIC FLAGPOLE

The Dutch purchased Manhattan Island from the Indians near this location in 1626 for $24 worth of trinkets. The main problem with this transaction is; What exactly transpired here? These Indians were not even from Manhattan. They were the Canarsie Indians, from Brooklyn, who were out on a hunting party and came upon these Dutch settlers who wanted to give them trinkets (shmah'tes) for land which they didn't even own? Anyway, the flagpole shows a relief of this transaction. There are two inscriptions–one side in Dutch and the other side in English.

Turn right at the flagpole and you come to...

Stop 11.
SUBWAY KIOSK

The Interborough Rapid Transit (IRT) was financed by the noted banker August Belmont. The name Belmont in French means "beautiful mountain." He changed his original family name from Schonberg, which in German means "beautiful mountain," to its French counterpart.

He specified that the new subway should be decorated with ornate mosaic tiles and terra cotta works of art. Each station was to be designed in a unique motif. This aided many hundreds of thousands of newly-arrived immigrants who could not read or speak English. So when they arrived at the Fulton Street station, they saw a terra cotta relief of Robert Fulton's Clermont sailing down the Hudson River. They knew that they had to get off the train at the station "with the boat."

The masonry kiosk was designed in 1905, as part of the Brooklyn extension of the subway, by Heins & La Farge in the Beaux-Arts style. It has recently been restored.

For a glimpse of the most unique and beautiful subway station try to see the one underneath City Hall. It was the first station of the IRT and is built on a hair-pin curve. The ceilings are arched and contain chandeliers and skylights, once decorated with stained-glass. This station will be open to the general public in a few years and will be part of the New York Transit Museum (now located in downtown Brooklyn).

But for now, when you come to today's Brooklyn Bridge station (southbound only), the #6 line terminates there. All passengers are requested to get off the train. If you can, try to stay on. The train usually makes a U-Turn and comes back on the uptown side of the same station. Along this U-Turn, the train passes by the old ghostly City Hall station. It appears very briefly on the right side of the train.

Cross the street and you will be at...

Stop 12.
U.S. CUSTOM HOUSE

Before there was an income tax, the duty levied on imported goods financed most of the federal budget. A good 80% of that duty came from the Port of New York. The U.S. Custom House was built in 1907 by Cass Gilbert in the Beaux-Arts style. The four statues sitting on pedestals along the main stairway were designed by Daniel Chester George and symbolize the four major continents; Asia, America, Europe and Africa. The oval rotunda contains murals by Reginald Marsh, commissioned as a WPA project in the 1930s.

The building stood empty for many years. At one time there were plans on turning the building into New York's Holocaust Museum. Those plans were rejected since the space was much too "ornate" for such a museum. The building was purchased by the Smithsonian Institute and now houses the National Museum of the American Indian, Tel. (212) 668-6624.

The upper and basement levels of the old U.S. Custom House still contain the U.S. Bankruptcy Court.

Just in front of the old U.S. Custom House is...

Stop 13.
BOWLING GREEN

This is New York's earliest park. the fence was erected by the Common Council in 1771. The park was leased in 1783 for use as a Bowling Green at a rental of one peppercorn a year. Patriots, who in 1776 destroyed an equestrian statue of King George III of England which stood here, are said to have removed the crowns which capped the fence posts but the fence itself remains.

Just north of Bowling Green, up the street is...

Stop 14.
CHARGING BULL

This monstrous sculpture by Arturo DiModica was "dumped" in front of the New York Stock Exchange in 1989, without any city permits. It was finally given this spot , at the southern tip of Broadway and is photographed by every tourist in town.

Cross Broadway and come to...

Stop 15.

No. ONE BROADWAY

Adjoining this site was the first Dutch fort on Manhattan Island known as Fort New Amsterdam. The first house was erected here before 1664. In 1771, Captain Archibald Kennedy built his residence here. It was used in 1776 by General George Washington as his headquarters and later by General Howe during the British occupation. It was later used as a hotel but was torn down. In 1882, it was replaced by the Washington Building which was transformed into the International Mercantile Marine Company and known as No. One Broadway.

The ground floor of the building is now occupied by a Citibank branch. Notice the signs over the two doorways (under the canopies) along Battery Place. One says, "First Class" and the other says "Cabin Class." This refers to First- and Cabin-Class ship passengers. This is where steamship tickets were purchased when the building was owned by the United States Lines.

Cross Battery Place to Battery Park, walk along all the tour buses and go towards the white pyramid. You have reached...

Stop 16.

MUSEUM OF JEWISH HERITAGE
A LIVING MEMORIAL TO THE HOLOCAUST

The newest museum in New York City opened September 15, 1997. It is organized around three basic themes: Jewish Life a Century Ago; The War Against the Jews; and Jewish Renewal. More than two thousand photographs and eight hundred historical and cultural artifacts convey the Jewish experience from the 1880s to the present. Twenty-four original documentary films chronicle the memories of survivors and include testimonies from Steven Spielberg's Survivors of the Shoah Visual History Foundation.

The 30,000 square foot museum's symbolic six-sided shape and tiered roof is a reminder of the six million who perished in the Holocaust, as well as the Star of David. The steeped louvered roof rises 85 feet in the air. The Museum of Jewish Heritage was designed by Kevin Roche John Dinkeloo & Associates.

Admission is $7 for adults and $5 for seniors and students. It is highly recommended to make reservations through TicketMaster at (212) 307-4007. For further information about the museum call (212) 968-1800.

Museum of Jewish Heritage is in viewing distance of Ellis Island.

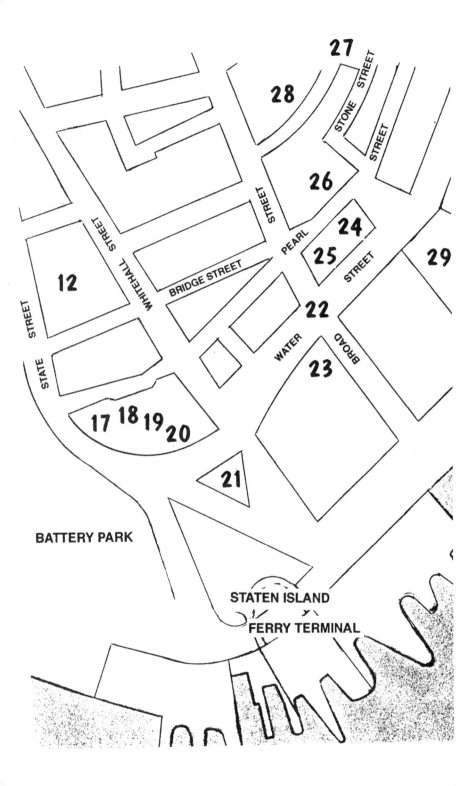

Walk back towards the old U.S. Custom House. At State Street, turn right or just follow the perimeter of Battery Park until you see a magnifi - cent sleek curved stainless steel skyscraper. You have reached...

Stop 17.

17 STATE STREET

This sleek curved skyscraper was designed by Emery Roth & Sons. Its futuristic design is the scene of "photo shoots" by ad agencies and fashion designers. There are mysterious laser light shows emanating from the penthouse in the evenings.

In the back plaza of 17 State Street are two exciting points of interest...

Stop 18.

BIRTHPLACE OF HERMAN MELVILLE

This is the site of the novelist and poet Herman Melville's birthplace. He was best known for his novel, *Moby Dick*. He was born here in 1819 and died in 1891.

Stop 19.

NEW YORK UNEARTHED

This is the only museum dedicated to New York's archaeological heritage, where remains of the past tell the story of New York's history. Visitors can view vestiges of early city life, dating from prehistoric times to the 1950s, unearthed from beneath the city streets, and watch conservators at work on the restoration of newly discovered treasures. Some of the items on display are Delft tiles from Holland, clay pipes, tenement medicine bottles, and children's dolls from the early 20th century. This museum is a branch of the South Street Seaport Museum.

The museum is open Monday through Saturday (no Saturdays from Jan. 1 - March 31) 12:00 - 6:00 pm. For further information call (212) 748-8628.

Go back to State Street and follow the curved street until you get to...

Stop 20.

JAMES WATSON TOWNHOUSE

The small house at 7 State Street, with columns supporting a portico, dates from 1793. Those double-story wooden columns were originally from a ships' masts. The Federal style building is today owned by the Shrine of St. Elizabeth Ann Seton. Mother Seton was canonized as America's first saint in 1975.

Cross the street and go the small triangular park. Proceed to the flagpole and notice...

Stop 21.

JEWISH PLYMOUTH ROCK

In commemoration of the first Jewish settlement in New York City, the copper marker states, "Erected by the State of New York to honor the memory of the twenty-three men, women and children who landed in September 1654, and founded the first Jewish community in North America." The oldest congregation in North America is still in operation. Congregation Shearith Israel, also known as the Spanish and Portuguese Congregation, is located at 8 West 70th Street in Manhattan. For information about the congregation call (212) 873-0300.

Walk along Water Street for one block until you reach...

Stop 22.

THE GRAND CANAL

The Dutch settlers of New Amsterdam wanted their colony to be "just like home." Holland consists of thousands of canals running through all cities, villages and even the countryside. Broad Street was a drainage and shipping canal. It was named after its prototype which can still be found in Amsterdam, the Heren Gracht or the "Male" or "Grand" Canal. There is an historic bronze marker on the floor behind 85 Broad Street which depicts a map of the area as it appeared under Dutch rule in 1660. The Heren Gracht went as far as today's Exchange Place. The original canal was filled one hundred years before the American Revolution.

Other points of interest in the area are some of the street names...

- **Bridge Street**
  is where an ancient bridge crossed over the Heren Gracht.
- **Stone Street**
  was the first street to be cobbled.
- **Pearl Street**
  was the shoreline of the East River. It was   filled with shells (Mother-of-Pearl).

• **Broad Street**
was so named because it was the "widest" street in New Amsterdam.
• **Water Street**
was once part of the East River.

Stop 23.

SUPREME COURT OF THE UNITED STATES

The corner of today' Water and Broad Streets was the site of the first Supreme Court of the United States. It convened at this site on February 2, 1740 in the Merchant's Exchange Building which formerly stood in the center of Broad Street. Chief Justice John Jay attended and presided in black and scarlet robes.

On November 3, 1789, the United States District Court also was convened here, following its establishment under the Judiciary Act of 1789, thus becoming the first court organized under sovereignty of the newly-formed national government. James Duane, who served as mayor of New York following the British evacuation, was appointed by General Washington to sit as the First District U.S. Judge.

Notice the street signs on each corner of the intersection of Water and Broad Streets. Some signs are green with white lettering while others are reddish brown with white lettering. The brownish-colored signs throughout the City of New York signify that this part of a city block has been designated an official historic landmark.

Look across the street and notice a cluster of four-story 18th and 19th century brick buildings...

Stop 24.

FRAUNCES TAVERN HISTORIC BLOCK

The Fraunces Tavern Historic Block is a rare example of a complete city block of 18th and 19th century buildings that had survived Lower Manhattan's successive waves of construction.

The block was under water when the Strand or Pearl Street was the original shorefront. The small stream that flowed down what is presently Broad Street emptied into the East River at Pearl Street.

In the end of the 17th century the tip of Manhattan Island had become such a busy shipping area that wharves and landfill extended the shoreline. By 1766, a strip of land two blocks deep had been added to the city.

In the 18th century wealthy homes, warehouses and some combined business and residential structures were located here. Pearl Street was widened in the 1820s, and residential buildings in the area gave way to more stores, factories and warehouses.

In the mid-19th century industry moved northward, and with the coming of steamships, shipping shifted to the wider Hudson River. In general, this area became a backwater area of stores, saloons and services for sailors. The Fraunces Tavern block buildings, however, continued as warehouses and light manufacturing plants.

After the 1929 stock market crash the docks were idle and more companies relocated to midtown. The area remained unchanged from the mid-19th century until the late 1950s, when a new construction boom began. Water Street was widened, and older blocks like this one came tumbling down to make way for new office towers.

The current buildings on the block represent a variety of eighteenth century styles, including Georgian, late Federal, Greek Revival and Victorian.

Cross Water Street and go up Broad Street for one block. That yellow brick building with the flags is...

Stop 25.

FRAUNCES TAVERN

Fraunces Tavern was originally built as a residence by Stephan de Lancey in 1719. Phila Franks, a descendant of the first Jewish settlers who arrived in 1654, married this non-Jew, Oliver de Lancey (as in Delancey Street, in today's Lower East Side). The mansion was converted into an inn which was later purchased by Samuel Fraunces, a West Indian innkeeper. In 1762, he opened the Queen's Head Tavern, which quickly became a gathering place for the Sons of Liberty and other patriots. A group of merchants met here in 1768 to establish the Chamber of Commerce.

During the Revolution, Samuel Fraunces was taken prisoner by the British. He spent the remainder of the war as a cook in the house of General James Robertson.

When the British evacuated the city on November 25, 1783, Governor Clinton hosted a celebration banquet at the tavern for George Washington and Chevalier de la Luzerne, France's Ambassador to the fledgling nation.

The tavern was also the scene of a more poignant gathering on December 1, 1783, when Washington met his officers here to bid them farewell. He then departed for Annapolis to resign his commission and return to his Mount Vernon home. In 1785. Samuel Fraunces sold the tavern. He was asked to join Washington's staff after Washington became President. The tavern was later used by the new nation's Department of Foreign Affairs and War Department.

In the end of the 19th century, the building was used as a meeting place for social, civil and service organizations. It was damaged by fire three times. A flat roof was added in 1832 and two additional stories were added in 1852. In 1904, it was acquired by the Son of the Revolution and in 1907 it was totally reconstructed by architect William H. Mersereau. It was again modified in 1927. The building used to look exactly like its adjoining warehouse structures. The architects envisioned a Federal style for Fraunces Tavern—so what you see today is a "mock-up" of the original building. In the 1970s, Fraunces Tavern was bombed during lunch-hour by the Puerto Rican Liberation Army. Several people were killed in this terrorist attack.

Fraunces Tavern today contains a restaurant on the first floor and a museum on the second level. For further information call (212) 425-1778.

Before moving on to the next site, take a look at the historic copper and bronze plaques on the outside corner of Fraunces Tavern. That's right, they are bolted down with steel brackets! This is New York afterall. People have already come in the middle of the night and literally ripped off historic metal plaques.

Cross Pearl Street and walk to the right in that little plaza. Look for the raised brick platform and then look at the railings. You have reached...

Stop 26.
ARCHAEOLOGICAL DIG

When construction workers were digging up the site for a massive sky-scraper which would occupy 85 Broad Street, work was halted because they hit some archaeological ruins. Archaeologists were called in to investigate the remains. After removing many of the finer items which have been put on display in the small museum at 17 State Street, New York Unearthed, the remaining foundation stones of Governor Lovelace's Tavern were left intact and covered over with clear glass. So now, the public can view a bit of original New York.

The first large scale archaeological excavation in New York City was conducted on this block in 1979-80. The excavation yielded important cultural material from the 17th through 19th centuries, proving that significant archaeological deposits can be found in heavily developed urban areas. A number of wells, privies (outhouses) and cisterns from the back-yards of early houses, and the foundations and associated materials from the Lovelace Tavern were discovered. Excavations under Stone Street also uncovered a series of earth surfaces dating from the 17th through 19th centuries.

The archaeological exhibit in the plaza at 85 Broad Street includes information about the Stadt Huys, Governor Lovelace's Tavern, an 18th century well and Stone Street, a 17th century thoroughfare. Present day Pearl Street represents the approximate 17th century shoreline of the East River.

GOVERNOR LOVELACE'S TAVERN

The Lovelace Tavern was built in 1670 under the directive of Francis Lovelace, the second English Governor of New York, and remained in use until 1706, when it was torn down. It was owned by the British Crown and served as a temporary city hall for a short time after 1697, when the first City Hall, the Stadt Huys, was declared unsafe for use.

Look down at the glass-covered excavation. You will see original foun-dation stones. Follow those stones to the edge of the glass enclosure to the brick floor of the plaza. The plaza is designed with brown herring-bone-patterned bricks. The solid gray granite stones on the floor repre-sent the outline of the entire foundation stones of Governor Lovelace's Tavern. They meet-up with the original foundation stones under the glass-enclosed excavation.

STADT HUYS

The Stadt Huys or City Hall in Dutch, was built as a tavern, the Stadt Herbergh (or City Inn), in 1641 by Director-General Kieft of the Dutch West India Company. When New Amsterdam became a municipality in 1653, the tavern was designated for use as the first City Hall, making it the center of governmental and political life in the colony. It continued to serve this municipal function under both Dutch and English rule until it was declared unsafe for use in 1697, and was later torn down. The city government then convened at several taverns, including Lovelace Tavern, until the new City Hall was built at the northeast corner of Wall and Nassau Streets in 1699.

Walk around the plaza, turn left, and at the back entrance to 85 Broad Street, look on the floor and see a map of New Amsterdam, showing Fort New Amsterdam and the Heren Gracht (Grand Canal).
Go up the stairs and walk into what looks like an alley. That is Stone Street. Walk one block to Mill Lane, turn left. Go to the corner and look at the new building on the right. There used to be an historic plaque at this location but it was removed. Anyway, you are at...

Stop 27.
FIRST JEWISH SETTLEMENT

In 1654, the first Jews arrived in New Amsterdam. Included in this group was Abraham de Lucena, who lived on this site until 1660. Asser Levy was the butcher and *mohel* (ritual circumcisor). He had a house on Mill Lane. He was also involved in real estate and owned properties in upstate New York (then known as *New Netherlands*) and in *Breukelen* (today's Brooklyn). He and other Jews later had homes and shops on adjacent Stone Street.

You are now at the intersection of Mill Lane and South William Street. If you turn right, you will see the old brownstone building on the next corner. That's the old Delmonico's Restaurant. Turn left onto South William Street. The first building on the corner, the white limestone Gothic Revival structure, was the first headquarters of Lehman Brothers. The next building, designed in 1908 in Flemish Revival, with its orange bricks and gabled roof, is a replica of what all of Dutch New Amsterdam looked like in its heyday. Cross the street and go to the Lincoln Square Parking Garage and...

Stop 28.
NORTH AMERICA'S FIRST SYNAGOGUE

The Jewish community worshiped on South William (originally called Mill) Street in a rented house until they erected the first synagogue in North America there in 1730. The plot of ground was purchased by Lewis and Mordecai Gomez, Jacob Franks and Rodrigo Pacheco, trustees of Congregation Shearith Israel, on behalf of the colonial Jewish community. The building was completed by 1730 and consecrated by the congregation on April 8 of that year. The construction of the synagogue marked the establishment of a permanent place of worship for the community.

The congregation later moved to Crosby Street, West 19th Street and finally to its present location on the Upper West Side, at 8 West 70th Street. The congregation is also known as the Spanish and Portuguese Synagogue.

There are three cemeteries which belong to this congregation. They are located on St. James Place, near Chatham Square in Chinatown; on West 11th Street, just east of Sixth Avenue; and on West 21st Street, just west of Sixth Avenue.

The earliest tombstone in the Chatham Square cemetery dates back to 1683.

There used to be an historic plaque indicating that this was the site of North America's first synagogue. It was located on the wall of the parking garage. One day it just vanished. It has not been replaced.
Cross South William Street, go through the split-level plaza behind 85 Broad Street, which is also called Coentis Slip. At one time the Third Avenue El made a hairpin S-turn through Coentis Slip and up Water Street. Cross over Water Street and you have arrived at...

Stop 29.
VIETNAM VETERANS MEMORIAL

North America's first synagogue was located on Mill Street.

New York City's first Vietnam Memorial is located in Jeannette Park, between Water and South Streets. It was erected in 1985 to commemorate the over-sixty thousand soldiers who died in that war. The memorial wall is composed of granite and glass-blocks. It is 14 feet high and 70 feet wide. The wall is inscribed with fragments of letters written by soldiers on the front to their loved ones. At night, the glass-blocks all illuminated from within.

Walk back to Broad Street, turn right and proceed up the hill to Wall Street. On your left is...

Stop 30.
NEW YORK STOCK EXCHANGE

Wall Street is named for the wooden fence which protected the settlers of the Dutch colony of New Amsterdam from Indian and British raids from the north. It was put up in 1653. The British took it down when they captured New Amsterdam in 1664, but the name "wall" street remained.

The New York Stock Exchange was organized in 1792 when merchants met informally under an old buttonwood tree on the sidewalk outside 68 Wall Street. One of the founders of the New York Stock Exchange was Ephraim Hart who was an American soldier and patriot and member of Congregation Shearith Israel, America's oldest synagogue. The New York Stock Exchange is the central marketplace for the purchase and sale of securities. The present building was completed in 1903 and was designed by George B. Post. Sculptors of the pediment were J.A.Q. Ward and Paul W. Bartlett. There are free tours of the Visitors' Gallery. For further information call (212) 656-5167.

You are now being watched! There are several cameras mounted on build - ing ledges, monitored by FBI agents, watching the streets around the New York Stock Exchange, for possible terrorist activities (since the bombing of the World Trade Center Towers). Big Brother is Watching, so just act cool...

Diagonally across the street from the New York Stock Exchange is...

Stop 31.
FEDERAL HALL NATIONAL MONUMENT

Throughout the 18th century, this was the vital center of New York's greatest events. At this place, the government of the United States of America began to function on Wednesday, March 4, 1789. New York City was the first capital of the United States, and New York City Hall—remodeled, enlarged and renamed Federal Hall in honor of its new national importance—was the first Capitol, the building in which Congress met for its first session, with the first Senate in one wing and the first House of Representatives in the other.

On April 30, 1789, George Washington took the oath of office on the balcony of Federal Hall and became the first President of the United States.

The original City Hall was built in 1703 at the north end of Broad Street. The city's population was less than five thousand, including one thousand Indians and slaves. Wall Street, which ran from river to river, was the northern boundary of the thickly built up area. Except for City Hall, Trinity Church and a handful of houses, everything had been built south of a protective wooden wall which was built by the Dutch in 1653.

The old Federal Hall was in a state of ruins after 1812. In 1842, the U.S. Customs House was built on this site in Greek Revival style by Town & Davis, with John Frazee and Samuel Thompson. In 1862, it became the Subtreasury Building. In 1955, Federal Hall was established as a national memorial. It is administered by the National Park Service.

At this point, the tour splits in two separate directions. Turn left at the corner of Broad and Wall Streets and see...

Stop 32.
TRINITY CHURCH

Trinity Church, one of the most historic buildings in the city, was established in 1697 by Royal Charter of King William III of England. Three churches have occupied the site on Broadway at the head of Wall Street. The first was opened in 1698, having been paid for by personal subscriptions and taxation of citizens regardless of creed. The Church of England was the colony's established religion. The original church, a modest structure with a small entrance porch, faced the Hudson River.

For seventy years Trinity Parish was the only Church of England Parish in Manhattan. The growing population was accommodated by the erection of St. George's Chapel in 1752 and St. Paul's Chapel in 1766.

Early in the Revolutionary War, the rector and vestrymen, many of whom were Tories, closed Trinity Church to Washington's army chaplains. It was reopened briefly when the British occupied New York but was destroyed in the Great Fire of 1776. Its ruins became known as "Burnt Church."

After the War of Independence, Trinity Church became part of the newly organized Protestant Episcopal Church in the United States. In 1788, the second church was begun on the site, and two years later it was consecrated in the presence of President Washington. It stood until 1839,

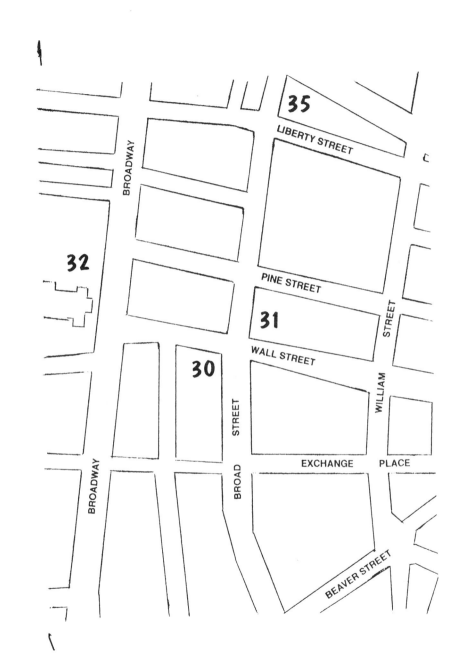

when heavy snows damaged the roof and the building was found to be structurally unsound.

The present Trinity Church was completed in 1846 from a design by architect Richard Upjohn. Its details are based on English Perpendicular Gothic prototypes. The spire was once the highest structure on the New York skyline. The tower contains ten bells; three of the eight original bells (a gift from London in 1797) are still in use. The bronze doors were designed by architect Morris Hunt.

The two-and-one-half-acre churchyard was a burial ground even during the Dutch period. Buried here are Alexander Hamilton (first Secretary of the Treasury), Albert Gallatin (member of Congress and Secretary of the Treasury for Jefferson), Francis Lewis (the only signer of the Declaration of Independence buried in Manhattan), Captain James ("Don't Give Up the Ship!") Lawrence, and Robert Fulton (a successful portrait painter as well as an inventor).

The Martyrs' Monument, a notable architectural feature of the churchyard, was erected in memory of the men who sacrificed their lives in the War of Independence.

Continue walking west, towards the Hudson River, to the Twin Towers...

Stop 33.

WORLD TRADE CENTER

The two 110-story towers were once the tallest in the world (before the Sears Tower in Chicago and an even taller one in southeast Asia were constructed). They were designed in 1966 by Minoru Yamasaki with Emery Roth & Sons. There are seven buildings in the complex, two hundred elevators and ten million square feet of office space accommodating 50,000 workers and 80,000 tourists each day. The World Trade Center is operated by the Port Authority of New York and New Jersey. There is a PATH subway terminal eight floors below street level. These trains service commuters to New Jersey.

The "Top of the World" observation deck on the 110th floor offers one of the best views of New York City and its surroundings. On a clear day you can see as far as forty miles away! For further information call (212) 323-2340.

Keep on walking west, cross over West Street (take the enclosed pedestrian bridge) and you come to a whole new city...

Stop 34.

WORLD FINANCIAL CENTER

Battery Park City consists of 92 acres of landfill. Much of this landfill comes from the excavations for the World Trade Center. The 14-acre

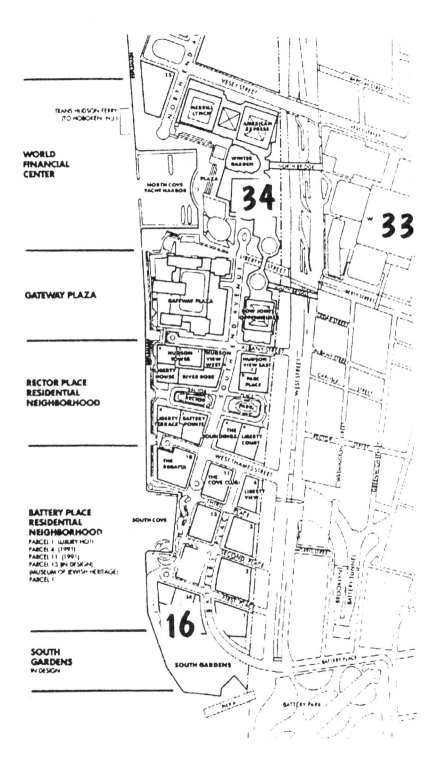

WORLD
FINANCIAL
CENTER

GATEWAY PLAZA

RECTOR PLACE
RESIDENTIAL
NEIGHBORHOOD

BATTERY PLACE
RESIDENTIAL
NEIGHBORHOOD
PARCEL 1 LUXURY HOTEL
PARCEL 4 (1991)
PARCEL 11 (1991)
PARCEL 13 (IN DESIGN)
(MUSEUM OF JEWISH HERITAGE)
PARCEL 1

SOUTH
GARDENS
IN DESIGN

World Financial Center was built by the Toronto-based Olympia & York Company.

The World Financial Center was designed by architect Cesar Pelli. The glazed *Wintergarden* is a grand public space comparable in size to Grand Central Station in New York. It has restaurants at its sides, and a grand staircase at its east forming a natural amphitheater for watching not only performances but the Hudson River as well.

The steel structure recalls industrialized structures of the 19th century. Sixteen palm trees, selected for having foliage only above eye level at the *Wintergarden's* second story, grow in aerat
ed soil and with the help of grow lamps. The 45-foot-high palm trees were brought from the Mohave Desert in California and can resist the low winter humidity, unlike tropical palms.

To accommodate the planters, the area beneath the *Wintergar-den,* which includes New Jersey PATH trains and, in fact, water from the Hudson River, had to be elaborately restructured. A "table" was built over the PATH tubes. The *Wintergarden* actually "sits" on this concrete table.

There are more than six acres of marble in 27 different varieties in the lobby floors and some wall areas, all of it hand-set by fifty stone cutters. An Italian quarry was even reopened to furnish one of the marbles. Both the gilt stenciled ceilings of the gatehouse building and the Scalamandre jacquard fabric on elevator core walls are examples of luxuries deemed worthwhile by Olympia & York's quality engineers.

Other major projects developed by Olympia & York include Toronto's *Harbourfront* and the *Canary Wharf* (the Docklands Project) in London's East End.

We will now go back to our split-off point, at the corner of Broad and Wall Streets. Walk up the narrow street to the left of Federal Hall (which becomes Nassau Street). Go one long block until you arrive at Liberty Street. You have come to...

Stop 35.
FEDERAL RESERVE BANK

The Federal Reserve Bank contains one fourth of the world's gold bullion reserves. The architects, York and Sawyer, had to excavate the entire block down to bedrock, as deep as 117 feet below street level (five stories) and 60 feet below sea level. The reason for such deep excavations was because only solid bedrock could support the enormous weight of the gold that would ultimately be stored in the depths of the building.

There are 122 compartments, representing countries from around the entire world. When a gold payment is paid from one country to another, the gold is never transported out this building. Instead, the gold is physically transferred on carts from one compartment to another in the same building.

In recent years, there have been several unsettling questions about gold transactions conducted by the Nazis and several neutral countries such as Switzerland, Spain and Portugal.

The architects modeled the Federal Reserve Bank after an Ital-ian Renaissance Strozzi *palazzo* in Florence, run by the Medicis. The luxurious iron lantern was designed by Samuel Yellin. The Federal Reserve Bank was completed in 1924. There are free 40-minute tours given Monday through Friday at 10:30, 11:30, 1:30 and 2:30. For reservations call (212) 720-6130.

Walk down the hill on Maiden Lane for three blocks to Water Street. Turn left and walk to Fulton Street. On the way you will see...

Stop 36.

127 JOHN STREET

This skyscraper was designed by Emery Roth & Sons. When the builders of the skyscraper were buying up the properties before construction, the John Street Restaurant refused to sell. The architects designed their skyscraper "around" the restaurant. In order to camouflage the blank wall of the three-story restaurant, the architects designed a digital wall clock rising the full height of the restaurant wall. The clock contains sixty numbers and illuminates the hours, minutes and seconds as they progress. So, if it's 12:30 and twenty seconds, the 12, the 30 and the 20 boxes would be illuminated.

The building is presently undergoing extensive renovations, so the clock isn't working. There used to be a metallic "tubular" entranceway, with purple neon lights encircling the inner tube. You felt as if you were entering a space station. The elevators had bright red neon lights. It was as if you were stepping into an X-Ray machine. On the "mechanical floors" (the 13th level and the penthouse level) where all of the building's plumbing, electrical, heating and air conditioning machinery were housed, there were bright "rainbows of color." Each machine apparatus was painted a bright primary color. There were also flickering "Christmas" lights which could seen from street level. On the street level, there was unique "street furniture" with sculptural designs and stage sets. In short, this was not your typical skyscraper. The architects had fun with it. Nobody knows, however, what the new owners of the building will do after the building is renovated.

At Fulton and Water Streets, before you turn right for the South Street Seaport, be sure to see the only memorial to the S.S. Titanic...

Stop 37.

TITANIC MEMORIAL

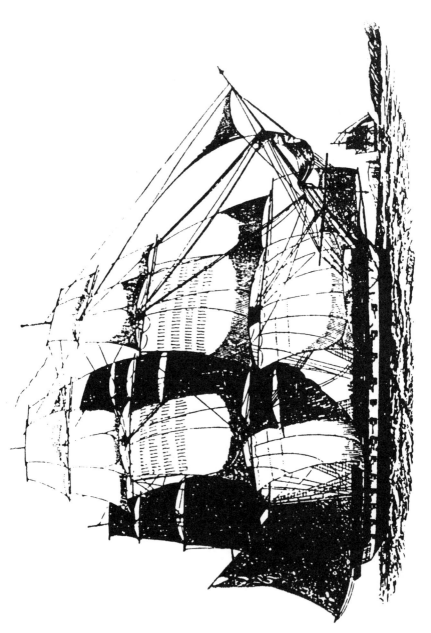

Clipper ship in full sail.

Located on the east side of Water Street, at the corner of Fulton Street, is the only memorial to the sinking of the *S.S. Titanic* in 1912. Fifteen hundred people drowned in that catastrophe, including Isador and Ida Straus, founders of Macy's Department Store. The memorial plaque is at the base of a lighthouse. The Titanic hit the iceberg on April 15, 1912 at 41 degrees 46' North, 50 degrees 14' West.

Stop 38.
SOUTH STREET SEAPORT MUSEUM

The South Street Seaport Museum celebrates old New York–the city that rose to world preeminence in the 19th century when South Street was known as the *Street of Ships*. Vessels of every description lined these East River piers, and seamen, immigrants, merchants and trades-men crowded these streets and buildings. Here was the center of the emerging city, the countinghouses and ship chandlieries, the sail lofts, printing establishments, sailors' bars and flophouses that animated the extraordinary contributions of maritime enterprise to the growth of American commerce and culture.

The South Street Seaport is a kaleidoscope of galleries, boutiques and shops as well as a tantalizing array of restaurants, cafes, eateries and markets. Stand on the balcony of Pier 17 and watch the harbor traffic of tugs and tankers pass under the Brooklyn Bridge–watch street perform-ers near the Fulton Fish Market–enjoy concerts on the piers, holiday fire-works or the singing Christmas tree.

See the *Seaport Experience* in New York's most unusual theater. Step aboard a 19th century tall ship, take a harbor cruise or come at 4:00 am, when the Fulton Fish Market comes to life.

Stop 39.
SCHERMERHORN ROW

The sloping roofs and tall chimneys of these early 19th century build-ings form the architectural centerpiece of the South Street Seaport. Built on speculation by Peter Schermerhorn, the block now contains restau-rants, a pub and many specialty shops. Once the whole neighborhood looked like this neat row of Federal and Greek Revival commercial build-ings.

Walk west along Fulton Street until you reach Broadway. You have reached...

Stop 40.
SAINT PAUL'S CHAPEL & GRAVEYARD

Saint Paul's Chapel was built in 1766 by Thomas McBean. Its model was James Gibb's masterpiece, the *Church of St. Martin-in-the-Field* in London. Stone from the site, Manhattan schist, forms the walls that are quoined, columned, parapeted, pedimented, porched and towered in brownstone. Governor Clinton's and President George Washington's pews are located in Saint Paul's Chapel.

The BMT "N" and "R" trains make a hairpin turn from Church Street to Broadway directly beneath the graveyard of Saint Paul's Chapel.

Walk two blocks northward along Broadway and come to...

Stop 41.
WOOLWORTH BUILDING

The Woolworth Building was designed in 1913 by Cass Gilbert in the Gothic style. He reproduced the Gothic spires, gargoyles, flying buttresses and lace-in-stone traceries. It was known as the *Cathedral of Commerce* and was the tallest building in the world until 1930. The three-story lobby contains a series of carved figures including Cass Gilbert holding a miniature model of the building; Louis Horowitz, the builder; Gunvald Aus, the steel engineer measuring a girder; and Frank W. Woolworth counting his nickels and dimes.

There are exterior statuary at the second story; bas relief heads representing Europe, Africa, Asia and America; and high above at the 26th, 49th and 51st floors, are carved gargoyles (bats, frogs, owls and pelicans) which crouch and gaze at the view.

The tower is constructed with portal braces, much like those at the ends of bridges, which conduct wind down to the ground instead of head-on into the building. The build-ing was designed to withstand winds as strong as 200mph.

The Woolworth Building soars 792 feet above the pavement and has 60 stories from sub-basement to tower. There are 30 acres of floor space, three thousand windows, 17 million bricks, 7500 tons of terra cotta, 28,000 tons of tile, and miles of marble wainscoting. The total cost was $13,500,000–*all paid in cash!*

Cross Broadway to...

Stop 42.
CITY HALL

City Hall was built in 1811 and was designed by Joseph F. Mangin and John McComb. This was one of the northernmost buildings in New York when it was constructed. The city-fathers felt that the city would not expand any further so they designed the front and side façades in mar-

The first subway station is located under City Hall.
Courtesy of the Transit Authority of New York

ble but the back of City Hall was faced with brownstone to save money!

The central hall, with its twin spiral, self-supporting marble stairs under a dome, is one of the finest public interiors. The Governor's Room was originally for his use when visiting New York City. It is now a portrait gallery.

Just below the front of City Hall is a magnificent arched subway station which opened in 1904. It will be converted into a branch of the New York Transit Museum in 1999. See *Stop 6.*

Just behind (to the north of) City Hall is...

Stop 43.
TWEED COURTHOUSE

The notorious *Tweed Ring* was involved in the construction of this building. It should have cost about $100,000 to construct the building which incorporated the finest marbles and crystal chan-deliers. It actually cost anywhere from $10 to $14 million to construct the Tweed Courthouse. It was built in 1872 and designed by John Kellum.

Keep walking northward. Cross Chambers Street and arrive at...

Stop 44.
SURROGATE'S COURT

The Surrogate's Court, located just across the street from the Tweed Courthouse, has been compared to a miniature version of the old Paris Opera House. It was designed in the Beaux-Arts style in 1911 by John R. Thomas, Horgan & Slattery.

Walk east on Chambers street to that tall building with an arched pas - sageway through it. That is...

Stop 45.
MUNICIPAL BUILDING

This magnificent skyscraper does not overwhelm the nearby City Hall. It was designed in 1914 by McKim, Mead & White. It is one of the few buildings that has a subway station running within its steel and concrete foundations. Chambers Street once continued *through* the building, under its glorious arch. The vaulted ceiling above the exterior courtyard was designed by the Guastavino Brothers.

Just behind the Municipal Building is...

Stop 46.

BROOKLYN BRIDGE

The Brooklyn Bridge was opened in 1883. It took sixteen years to build and cost the lives of more than twenty people, including that of its designer, John A. Roebling. The bridge was completed by his son, Washington A. Roebling. It is one of the most beautiful bridges in the world. In 1883, it connected two independent cities, New York and Brooklyn. Brooklyn is celebrating its Centennial–joining the City of New York in 1898.

The Gothic towers of the Brooklyn Bridge were the tallest structures in the city at the time of their construction. The skyscrapers of Lower Manhattan were not built until the late 1880s.

For great views of the harbor, take a leisurely stroll across the Brooklyn Bridge...
There is a detour at this point. Walk back to Broadway, turn right and walk seven blocks north from Chambers Street to White Street. Turn left and go to...

Stop 47.

A FLOATING SYNAGOGUE
49 White Street   Tel. (212) 966-7141

This synagogue is located just west of the Lower East Side, in a section called Tribeca. This refers to the **Tri**angle be**l**ow **Ca**nal Street. Congregation Shaare Zedek, the Civic Center Synagogue, was designed in 1967 by William Berger. It is nestled between two former sweatshop loft buildings. The synagogue seems to "float" between its two adjoining neighbors. Its design was inspired by the "scroll" of the Torah as it spreads open.

Walk back to Worth Street, turn left and go to Chatham Sqaure or (if you remained at Water Street under the Brooklyn Bridge) walk north along Water Street, which becomes Pearl Street north of the Brooklyn Bridge. Continue for about three blocks and look for a small park on the right side of the street. You have reached...

Stop 48.

OLDEST JEWISH CEMETERY

The first Jewish cemetery in the United States was consecrated in 1656 in New Amsterdam. The exact location of that cemetery is unknown. The remains of the cemetery were removed to the Chatham Square burial

The Civic Center Synagogue seems to float between two buildings.

Interior of the Civic Center Synagogue.

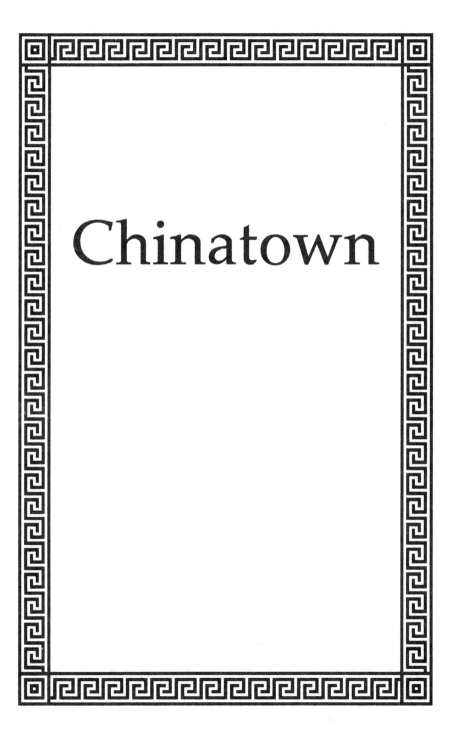

Chinatown

grounds. It was acquired in 1682. Benjamin Bueno de Mesquita, who died in 1683, was the first person to be buried there.

The cemetery played an important part in the American defense of New York in 1776. It was fortified by the patriots as one of the defenses of the city. Among the graves in the cemetery are those of 18 Revolutionary soldiers and patriots. These include Hayman Levy, Isaac Moses, and Gershom Mendes Seixas, minister of Congregation Shearith Israel, who closed the only synagogue in the city and removed the Torahs to Stratford, Connecticut, when British forces occupied New York.

This is one of three Jewish cemeteries in Manhattan which belong to North America's oldest congregation, Shearith Israel, also known as the Spanish and Portuguese Synagogue. The other two cemeteries are located on West 11th Street (just east of Sixth Avenue) and on West 21st Street (just west of Sixth Avenue).

Continue walking north to the large intersection, Chatham Square. Turn right onto East Broadway and go to No. 47.

Stop 49.

SITE OF RABBI ISAAC ELCHANAN THEOLOGICAL SEMINARY

Named after Rabbi Isaac Elchanan Spektor, a prominent scholar from Kovno, Lithuania, the Theological Seminary was the forerunner of today's Yeshiva University. It was organized in 1886 at 47 East Broadway, then moved to East Broadway and Montgomery Street, and is today located at its main campus in the Washington Heights section of Manhattan.

Walk east along East Broadway and proceed under the Manhattan Bridge. Turn left onto Forsyth Street. Go to the large church at No. 27...

Stop 50.

SAINT BARBARA GREEK ORTHODOX CHURCH

This building was originally designed as a synagogue, Congregation Mishkan Israel Suwalki, in 1895. The first distinct Jewish neighborhood arose in the 1870s at the corner of Bayard and Mott Streets (now in the heart of Chinatown). These people were skilled tailors from Suwalki and Great Poland (located near the German border). There is a red brick tenement structure at Bayard and Elizabeth Streets which displays Stars of David on its façade.

These Jews later moved to the area near Canal and Essex Streets. They organized a congregation during that period and built the magnificent synagogue at 27 Forsyth Street, just opposite today's Manhattan

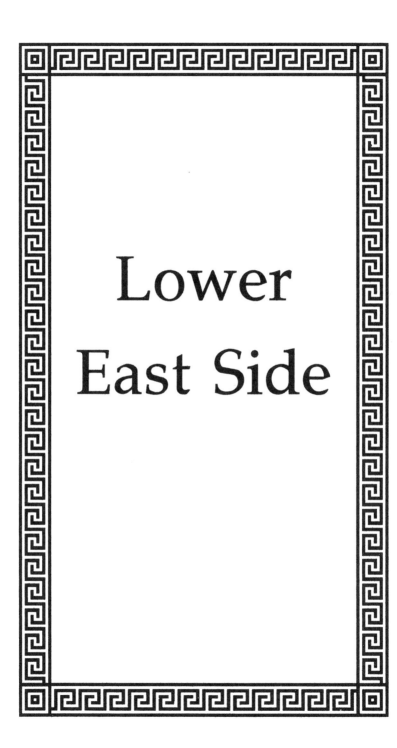

Lower
East Side

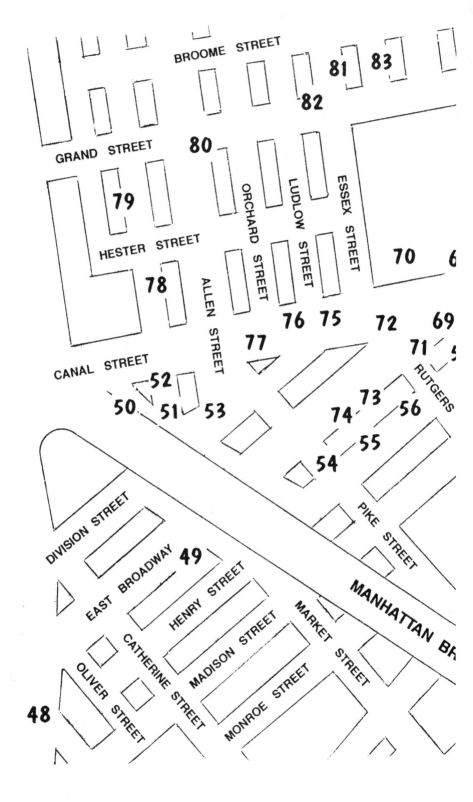

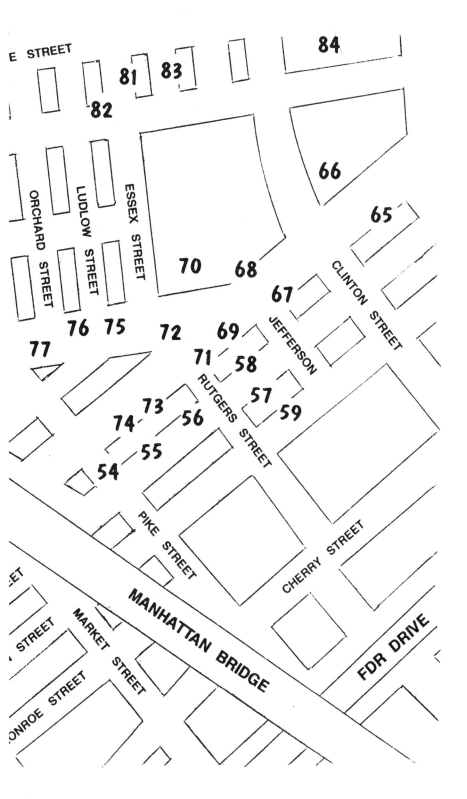

Bridge entrance. That building is still extant but is now used by Saint Barbara Greek Orthodox Church.

Double back to Division Street, turn left and make another left onto Eldridge Street, and proceed to No. 12

Stop 51.

ELDRIDGE STREET SYNAGOGUE

Built by Eastern European immigrants in 1886, the Eldridge Street Synagogue, Congregation Kahal Adas Jeshurun Anshei Lubz, was created by a merger of two congregations, Adas Jeshurun and Anshei Lubz. It was the first major Orthodox synagogue built specifically as a synagogue in the Lower East Side. Other congregations such as the Bialystoker Shul, the Roumaniashe Shul and the Beth Hamedrash Hagadol simply purchased former churches and converted them into synagogues.

Some of the founding fathers of the Eldridge Street Shul included Isaac Gellis (of hot-dog fame) and Sandor Jarmulowsky, noted for his high-rise bank building located at the corner of Orchard and Canal Streets. Yossele Rosenblatt was once the cantor of this synagogue. A young Eddie Cantor once sang in the choir of the Eldridge Street Shul. His home was located just across the street, at 19 Eldridge Street.

The synagogue was designed by the Herter Brothers. They also designed several tenement buildings in the late 1880s using their unique signature, Stars of David engraved on the façades. The architectural style of the Eldridge Street Shul is a mixture of Gothic, Romanesque and Moorish.

The main sanctuary is an immense and opulent hall with elaborate brass chandeliers with Victorian glass shades hanging in the middle of a huge barrel-vaulted space. The space is as glorious as the Great Synagogue in Florence, Italy. The Ark was designed in Italian walnut. The details on the Ark closely resemble those found on the Ark of Pittsburgh's Beth Hamedrash Hagadol Beth Jacob Congregation, which was built in 1873.

When the $8 million restoration project is completed, the Eldridge Street Synagogue will function as a synagogue/museum. There will be daily prayer services in the morning and evening. Other times, during "business hours," the synagogue will function as a Jewish museum with educational programs and tours, open to the general public.

There have been continuous weekly religious services in this synagogue since it was built in 1886. Even during major structural renovations, with steel beams reinforcing the ceiling of the *bais hamedrash* (daily chapel), there *were* Sabbath services. All participants in the minyan, however, were required to wear "hard hats" during the prayer services!

The Eldridge Street Synagogue was built in 1886.

The Eldridge Street Synagogue Restoration Project offers tours of the facilities for individuals and for groups. Admission is $4 for adults and $2.50 for seniors and students. For reservations and more information call (212) 219-0888.

The Eldridge Street Synagogue was declared a National Historic Landmark in 1996.

Cross the street and look at 19 Eldridge Street...

Stop 52.

HOME OF EDDIE CANTOR

Located directly across the street from the Eldridge Street Synagogue, is the tenement home of the radio and movie personality, Eddie Cantor. He took acting and voice lessons at the Educational Alliance (197 East Broadway) to improve his acting and singing career. His photograph is hanging in the lobby of that institution, on a wall called "Hall of Famers," along with other great personalities who took classes at the Educational Alliance. Just for fun, try to find a Star of David as part of a mosaic floor design in a nearby tenement entrance.

Go back to Division Street, turn left and go to the corner of Allen (Pike) Street...

Stop 53.

MANHATTAN RAILWAY COMPANY
ELECTRICAL SUBSTATION (former)
100 Division Street (NW corner Allen St.)

This facility served the Second Avenue El (elevated train) which ran from the Brooklyn Bridge, along Allen Street, turned at 23rd Street, and continued up along Second Avenue. It had a spur at 59th Street and crossed over the Queensboro Bridge. Part of that spur is visible at either end of the bridge. The Second Avenue El continued to the Bronx.

Allen Street was originally as narrow as Orchard and Ludlow Streets but was widened in 1930 by removing one section of tenements which faced Allen Street. When standing on Allen Street today, you can see only the "backs" of tenements which face Orchard Street.

Allen Street's perpetual darkness and noise from the Second Avenue El made it an undesirable place. It was once the city's most notorious "Red Light" district!

Turn right on Allen (which becomes Pike) Street and walk one block. Look diagonally across the street to that old gray limestone structure wedged between two apartment buildings...

Third Avenue El linked the Jewish communities of the Lower East Side, Harlem and the Bronx around the turn of the century.
Courtesy Merlis Collection

Stop 54.

PIKE STREET SHUL (former)

Congregation Sons of Israel Kalvarier was built at 15 Pike Street in 1903. It was once one of the great synagogues in the Lower East Side. The first ordination ceremony of the Rabbi Isaac Elchanan Theological Seminary was held in this synagogue in 1906. Ordination (s'micha) was granted to three rabbis. In 1917, this congregation had an uptown branch in Harlem. Harlem was a major Jewish area, with over 178,000 Jewish inhabitants during its peak period, in the 1910s.

More recently, the Pike Street Shul was the site of the funeral of Rav Aaron Kotler, prominent Torah scholar and rosh yeshiva (dean) of the Bais Hamedrash Gevohah in Lakewood. The funeral was attended by one hundred thousand people.

In the 1970s, the congregation had dwindled down to a handful of elderly members. Some moved to Florida. There was basically no one left to run the shul. So, several of the New York members decided to sell the shul to a local Chinese church, without the knowledge or permission of the other members of the congregation who had settled in Florida. The case was brought to litigation. After several years in the courts the judge ruled that the sale was null and void.

However, during those years of litigation, the building was totally neglected. Vandals broke in on a daily basis and took out any items which were of any value, e.g. brass fixtures, plumbing fixtures, etc. The building was basically abandoned. Drug addicts moved in and conducted their business.

At this point, the city took over the building, bricked-up the front doorways and sealed-up what was left of the elegant stained-glass windows. The building went up for auction. It was purchased by a local Chinese church.

Pike Street is now part of Chinatown and the old Pike Street Shul is now a Chinese church, with a hardware store on street level.

Walk along Pike Street, go to the corner of Henry Street. Turn left and proceed to 135 Henry Street...

Stop 55.

CHEVRE MISHKAN ANSHE ZETEL

This is one of the few remaining shteeblech (mini-synagogues) in the Lower East Side. It is located at 135 Henry Street.

Continue walking east along Henry Street to the next corner...

Stop 56.

SAINT TERESA'S ROMAN CATHOLIC CHURCH
16-18 Rutgers Street   Tel. (212) 233-0233

This building was erected as the First Presbyterian Church of New York in 1841, when the neighborhood was still a semi-rural suburb. In 1863, when the neighborhood was becoming heavily Irish, the building was purchased by the Archdiocese, and it has been a Roman Catholic church ever since. It now serves the Hispanic and Oriental groups of the neighborhood. Masses are conducted in Spanish, Chinese and English.

Continue going eastward on Henry Street...

Stop 57.

FORMER SYNAGOGUE
156 Henry Street

This building was built for Congregation Agudas Anshe Mamud u'Bais Va'ad Lachachamim in 1904. The congregation moved to the Home of the Sages at 283 East Broadway. It sold its original building to a Chinese church. The Stars of David are still visible in the large circular windows.

Directly across the street is...

Stop 58.

SITE OF YESHIVA RABBI JACOB JOSEPH
203 Henry Street

In 1899, Rabbi Jacob Joseph from Vilna, Lithuania, was appointed "Chief Rabbi" of the City of New York. This designation was met with much resistance and lasted only several months. He was also rabbi of the Beth Hamedrash Hagadol, located at 60 Norfolk Street.

The yeshiva or Hebrew school, named in his honor, was built in 1913 and was known as RJJ. It was one of the most prominent learning institutions in the city. In 1976, the yeshiva moved to Staten Island. The two buildings stood empty for several years. They were ultimately purchased by a developer who renovated them into residential apartments. The original Hebrew and English name entablatures of the yeshiva were left intact on the front façade.

The small playground just to the left of the former RJJ Yeshiva, on the corner of Rutgers Street, was named in memory of Captain Jacob Joseph, the grandson of the Chief Rabbi, who was killed-in-action as a United States Marine in Guadacanal during World War II.

Take a short detour around the corner. Go back to Rutgers Street, turn left and at the corner of Madison Street, make another left. Go to...

Stop 59.

FORMER SYNAGOGUE
209 Madison Street

This tenement-style synagogue belonged to Congregation Etz Chaim Anshe Volozin. It closed in 1989 and was renovated into residential apartments.

Return to Henry Street and proceed east to No. 263...

Stop 60.

HENRY STREET SETTLEMENT
263-267 Henry Street   Tel. (212) 766-9200

The Henry Street Settlement was founded in 1893 by Lilian Wald, the pioneer social worker. The agency was originally called the Nurses' Settlement. Lilian Wald was a nurse as well and organized what is still known today as the Visiting Nurse Service, which has assisted thousands of sick people in their homes.

The elegant Greek Revival town houses, built in 1832, were donated to the Henry Street Settlement by Jacob H. Schiff, one of the wealthiest and most prominent of the "Uptown" Jewish philanthropists associated with the Educational Alliance.

Note the exquisite town houses with dormers just around the corner, on Grand and Clinton Streets. They were built in the 1820s and 1830s.

Continue eastward to 290 Henry Street...

Stop 61.

SAINT AUGUSTINE'S CHAPEL
290 Henry Street   Tel. (212) 673-5300

Originally known as All Saints Church, it was built between 1827 and 1829 in the Federal style. Its fieldstone design is similar to the Willett Street Methodist Church, which was built in 1826 but is now used by the Bialystoker Synagogue.

This church was designed with an upstairs slave gallery into which black slaves were shackled while their white owners worshiped below. The original iron shackles were recently removed from the upper galleries.

The story is told of "Boss" William Marcy Tweed, who headed the infa-

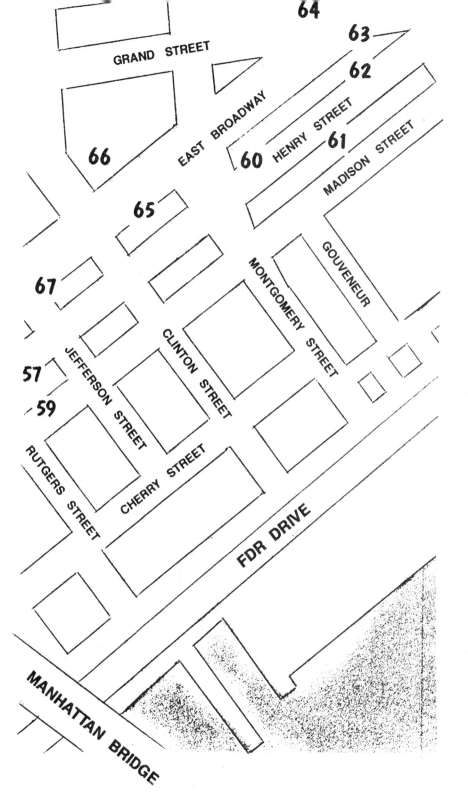

mous ring which drained New York City's treasury in the 1860s and 1870s. At the time of his mother's death, Tweed was a fugitive from justice, but nevertheless he attended her funeral in this church by hiding himself in the old slave gallery.

Cross the street and go to...

Stop 62.

EAST SIDE TORAH CENTER
313 Henry Street

This institution celebrated its 100th anniversary in 1990. There are several historic plaques along the building's façade commemorating this event.

Proceed to the corner. Make a left turn on East Broadway...

Stop 63.

EAST SIDE MIKVEH - RITUALARIUM
313 East Broadway   Tel. (212) 475-8514

Built in 1904 as the Arnold Toynbee Hall, this structure served as a settlement house which provided educational and recreational activities for the newly-arrived immigrants in the Lower East Side. The initials of the original institution "ATH" still appear in the stone balustrade over what had once been the main entrance.

The building later housed the Young Men's Benevolent Association. Recently, the building was purchased and restored by the nearby Gouverneur Hospital. It houses administrative offices.

The mikveh is still functioning as well. A mikveh or ritual bath is an important part of life for Orthodox Jewish women, who must attend as part of the preparation for marriage, and who are required to cleanse themselves in it every month.

Look across the street at the low-rise brown apartment buildings...

Stop 64.

AMALGAMATED DWELLINGS
Grand, Broome, Willett and Lewis Streets

The Amalgamated Dwellings are also known as the Sidney Hillman Houses. They were an early experiment in cooperative housing, built in 1930 under the auspices of the Amalgamated Clothing Workers of America. It has a central garden with a fountain. The scale is modest and humane, and the overall effect is altogether civilized and dignified. It was designed by the architectural firm of Springsteen and Goldhammer.

Walk west along East Broadway to...

Stop 65.

SHTEEBLE ROW
225-283 East Broadway

Between 1880 and 1924 more than two million Jews emigrated to New York City. They arrived with their entire families and, in some instances, with their entire communities. They established brotherly aid societies (*landsmanschaften*), burial societies and synagogues.

In its peak, around the turn of the century, the Lower East Side had over 600,000 Jewish immigrants and over five hundred synagogues. Many of these synagogues were not free-standing structures. Rather, they were apartments in tenements or renovated store-fronts converted into mini-synagogues. The term for such a small synagogue is *shteeble*, a Yiddish word meaning "small room."

The second section of this tourbook contains the master list of many of these small synagogues. Sometimes, as many as five or six separate congregations were housed in one tenement building. Some synagogues were named after the cities or villages (*shtetls*) in Eastern Europe. Other congregations were organized by various trades e.g. shoemakers, plumbers, tailors, etc., and were known by such names as the "*Tailor's Shul.*"

The question remains, "Why were there so many congregations?" The answer may lie in the classic tale of a shipwrecked castaway. After several years on a desert island, a ship came along and rescued this lone Jewish survivor and found an entire village, complete with shops, homes and two large synagogues. The captain asked the survivor, "Why were there two synagogues on this desert island." He replied as he pointed to each synagogue, "This is the synagogue that I pray in every single day. And that is the synagogue that I'll never set foot into!" That may be why there were over five hundred individual congregations in the Lower East Side around the turn of the century.

There are still about a dozen shteeblech along East Broadway, between Clinton and Montgomery Streets. One of these mini-synagogues was originally located on Cannon Street. It was relocated to East Broadway in the 1950s, when Cannon Street disappeared during an Urban Renewal Project—the construction of the Co-Ops. The sign in front of this shteebl therefore provides the name of the congregation (in Hebrew) with the key phrase, "*Formerly 52 Cannon Street.*"

Cross the street to that tall orange building...

Stop 66.

BIALYSTOKER HOME FOR THE AGED
228 East Broadway

Designed in the 1920s in the Art Deco style, the Bialystoker Home for the Aged houses many senior citizens who arrived in the Lower East Side in the early part of this century. The twelve entablatures around the front entrance are symbolic of the twelve tribes of Israel.

JEWISH MURAL

On the right side wall of the Bialystoker Home for the Aged is a mural designed in the 1970s by the Jewish art students of the Educational Alliance. The mural depicts the history of the Jewish people vis-a-vis the Lower East Side.

The upper left section of the mural depicts the immigrants arriving in New York on the ocean steamers in the late 1880s. Below that is a sign for the Jewish Daily Forward (*Forverts*, in Yiddish) which is still in publication. Below the sign is a rendering of labor union workers marching for better working conditions. Many of those rallies were held in Union Square, near 14th Street. Union Square is actually named for the Union Armies which assembled at that location and served as a staging point during the Civil War. A sister Union Square can be found in downtown San Francisco, which also served as a military staging point.

The mural depicts the logo of the International Ladies Garment Workers Union (ILGWU). That labor union, which was organized in the Lower East Side, is still functioning and was recently popularized by a catchy tune, *"Look for the Union Label..."*

The upper right section of the mural depicts victims of the Holocaust. The Star of David wrapped with chains is symbolic of the plight of the Soviet Jews. Since this mural was drawn in the 1970s, several hundred thousand Russian Jews have been allowed to leave Russia.

In the center of the mural is the focal point of the Jewish people–the State of Israel.

Proceed walking westward on East Broadway to...

Stop 67.

EDUCATIONAL ALLIANCE
197 East Broadway   Tel. (212) 475-6200

Organized in 1889, the Educational Alliance was the first settlement house in the United States created by the Jewish community. It was organized by the wealthy "Uptown Jews" –members of the German-Jewish community that had itself made the Lower East Side its original

Jewish mural next to the Bialystoker Home for the Aged.

home in the 1830s-1870s. These "Uptown Jews" felt an obligation to help out the newly-arrived Eastern European Jews who lived downtown, and wanted at the same time, to prevent anti-Semitism against their coreligionists. Some say that these "Uptown Jews" were also ashamed and embarrassed of these people who were dressed in the "Old World" garb and only spoke Yiddish.

The established German-Jewish community organized the Educational Alliance in order to quickly "Americanize" the new immigrants. There were classes in English, art, music, civics, theater, etc.

There were once huge bronze plaques in the lobby of the Educational Alliance honoring some of its founders. Some of these notable philanthropists included Louis Marshall, Jacob H. Schiff, Felix M. Warburg, Benjamin (B.) Altman and Isidor Straus. Straus was president of the board of trustees of the Educational Alliance from its founding in 1889 until 1912, when he and his wife went down with the *Titanic*. Isidor Straus was also the founder of Macy's Department Store.

The lobby contains its "Hall of Famers" –photographic portraits of distinguished alumni of the Educational Alliance including David Sarnoff, the young immigrant who learned English in its classes and later founded RCA; Arthur Murray, who practiced his first dance steps at Saturday night socials; Eddie Cantor, who acted and sang in theater productions; Jo Davidson and Jacob Epstein, who each paid three cents a week for lessons in sculpture and used as volunteer models the pushcart peddlers from nearby Orchard and Rivington Streets; and Chaim Gross, who took art classes here and later instructed art students of the Educational Alliance until his recent death at the age of 100. Some of Chaim Gross' lithographs are on display in the lobby.

Sholom Aleichem wrote many of his stories at a desk in the Alliance and, in 1906, appeared with Mark Twain in a joint lecture at the building's Isidor Straus Theater. The great Yiddish writer was introduced to the audience as the "Jewish Mark Twain"–to which Twain responded, "I am the American Sholom Aleichem."

The Educational Alliance is today run by the UJA-Federation and is basically a community center catering to the three dominant ethnic groups in the neighborhood; Jewish, Oriental and Hispanic. The locals call the Educational Alliance, the "*Edjees.*"

Continue walking westward...

Stop 68.

NEW YORK PUBLIC LIBRARY–SEWARD PARK BRANCH
192 East Broadway

This branch of the New York Public Library was built in 1909. At that time, the area was teaming with immigrants. Tenements were built right up against east side of the library. You can still see the "ghost" of the adjoining building on the right wall. The architects decided to give the immigrants a special area where they could read their books outdoors in the fresh air. A rooftop garden with exquisite copper railings and ornaments was constructed. That rooftop garden is now closed and is just an architectural detail.

This branch of the New York Public Library still has a large selection of books in Yiddish but also has books in Chinese and Spanish, catering to all of the ethnic groups in the neighborhood.

Proceed in this westward direction and look across the street at the tall structure...

Stop 69.

JEWISH DAILY FORWARD BUILDING
175 East Broadway

This section of East Broadway was once known as the "Publishers Row" of the Yiddish newspaper. Five Yiddish papers were once published on this street. The largest on the block, the Jewish Daily Forward (*Forverts* in Yiddish), was founded in 1897. Its publisher from 1903 to 1951 was Abraham Cahan. He introduced a special feature called "*A Bintel Brief*" or bundle of letters, the Yiddish equivalent to a "Dear Abby" column.

The Jewish Daily Forward building, one of the largest structures in the Lower East Side, also housed the headquarters of the Workmen's Circle (*Arbiter Ring* in Yiddish), as well as many other Jewish social and benevolent organizations and burial societies (*landsmanschaften*). The building was recently sold to a Chinese church. It has been designated an official New York City landmark. That means primarily that no part of the building's exterior façades may be altered. Therefore, the Yiddish name entablature at the top of the building, just below the clock, nor the Chinese lettering on the right side of the building which says, "*Jesus Saves,*" can never be removed.

The Jewish Daily Forward is still published, not as a daily paper but rather as a weekly edition. There are Yiddish and English editions of the paper. The paper and the Workmen's Circle are today located at 45 East 33rd Street, near Park Avenue.

Just a block to the left (east) of the old Jewish Daily Forward building on East Broadway is New York's other major Yiddish newspaper, the *Algemeiner Journal*. It recently returned to its roots in the Lower East Side.

Just opposite the Jewish Daily Forward Building is...

Top detail of the old Jewish Daily Forward Building.

Stop 70.

SEWARD PARK
East Broadway, Canal and Essex Streets

This vest-pocket park was created in 1900 by the demolition of two blocks of tenements. This park was the place where thousands of newly-arrived immigrants would gather each dawn. Owners of nearby sweatshops would come and randomly select workers for daily employment. This daily "shape-up" was known as the "*Chazir Mark,*" a Yiddish term referring to a pig market.

A mural of this artisan's market once appeared on the wall of the old Garden Cafeteria (now the Wing Shing restaurant-located at East Broadway and Rutgers Street). That mural was to be moved to the Jewish Museum but somehow "disappeared" during the transition of ownership of the restaurant from Jewish to Chinese.

Just opposite Seward Park is...

Stop 71.

GARDEN CAFETERIA (former)
165 East Broadway

This was the site of the landmark Jewish eatery, the Garden Cafeteria, until its sale to a Chinese restaurant in 1987. It was the meeting place for Yiddish writers, poets and actors from the 1920s through the 1960s.

This intersection is called...

Stop 72.

NATHAN STRAUS SQUARE
East Broadway, southeast corner Essex Street

This square is named in honor of Nathan Straus, the philanthropist who made it possible for the poor and young to have pasteurized milk, thereby saving thousands of lives. In 1920, there were 300 Nathan Straus milk stations throughout the United States.

Continue westward along East Broadway to...

Stop 73.

MESIFTA TIFERETH JERUSALEM
145 East Broadway   Tel. (212) 964-2830

One of the last surviving yeshivas or Hebrew schools in the Lower East Side, Mesifta Tifereth Jerusalem (MTJ), was organized by the Orthodox community around the turn of the century. It is an all boys school with classes from the kindergarten level through rabbinical seminary. Originally, the student body numbered close to one thousand. Now, there are only about 250 students in all classes. The main study hall or *bais hamedrash* also functions as a synagogue, with daily services.

The last *rosh yeshiva* or dean of Mesifta Tifereth Jerusalem was the world-renowned Torah scholar, Rabbi Moshe Feinstein. He passed away just before the holiday of Purim, on March 24, 1986. The funeral was held in the bais hamedrash, with an overflow crowd of thousands in the street outside. He was buried in Jerusalem.

There are several former yeshiva buildings in the area. The former Rabbi Jacob Joseph Yeshiva (RJJ) is located at 203 Henry Street. It moved to Staten Island in 1976. The former yeshiva buildings were renovated into residential apartments.

The old East Side Hebrew Institute, located at the corner of Avenue B and East 8th Street (opposite Tompkins Square Park), has also been converted into an apartment house.

Mesifta Tifereth Jerusalem has a branch on Staten Island. They purchased a former Catholic orphanage near the Outerbridge Crossing, at 1870 Drimgoold Road East, in the Princes Bay section.

The last yeshiva for girls in the Lower East Side, Beth Jacob, is located at 142 Broome Street.

Just right of Mesifta Tifereth Jerusalem is...

Stop 74.

JEWISH TENEMENTS
137-139 East Broadway

The Herter Brothers, a noted architectural firm, designed mansions along Fifth Avenue and the glorious Eldridge Street Synagogue in the Lower East Side. They were commissioned to design several tenement buildings specifically for the mass influx of Jewish immigrants in the late 1880s. The architects designed standard five-story walk-ups but initialed their buildings with terra cotta Stars of David motifs above the windows. These designs were never intended to signify that these buildings served a religious function but were rather just architectural ornamentations.

Other buildings designed by the Herter Brothers with similar Star of David motifs can be found at 47 Orchard Street and on Broome Street, between Mott and Mulberry Streets–in the heart of today's Little Italy! The last location has a splendid cornice designed with a sculpture of Moses.

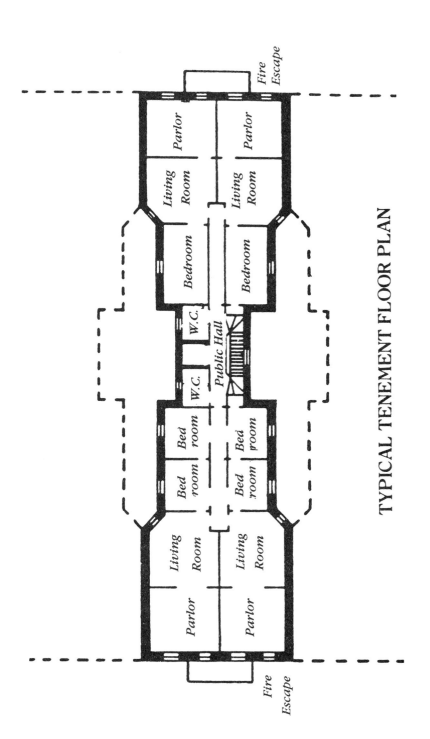

TYPICAL TENEMENT FLOOR PLAN

Double back along East Broadway to Nathan Straus Square. Turn left to Canal Street to...

Stop 75.

CANAL STREET THEATER (former)
31 Canal Street

The beautifully detailed terra cotta façade of the old Canal Street Theater can be seen at 31 Canal Street. It was once a silent movie palace, built in the 1920s. The auditorium of the theater, with its side exits and fire escapes, is still visible along the Ludlow Street façade.

The main lobby of the old movie palace now houses an electric appliance store (ABC Trading Co.). The original terra cotta ornaments in the lobby of the former movie palace are still visible along the high ceiling and the side walls. The main auditorium now houses a warehouse.

Walk to the next corner, Ludlow Street...

Stop 76.

KLETZKER
BROTHERLY AID ASSOCIATION (former)
5 Ludlow Street

Located across the street from the former Canal Street Theater is the former Kletzker Brotherly Aid Association. It was organized by a group of Jews who came from the city of Kletzk over one hundred years ago. This organization was known as a *landsmanschaft*–an association of people from the old town who could provide the lonely immigrant who might have just arrived without his family with moral support and funds for the basic necessities such as medical care or possibly for burial needs. Some brotherly aid societies assisted struggling businessmen or helped congregations build their own synagogues.

The building is no longer owned by the Kletzker Brotherly Aid Association, although the name entablature is still highlighted with a Star of David. The building is now utilized by a Chinese funeral parlor.

Walk west for one block along Canal Street...

Stop 77.

JARMULOWSKY'S BANK BUILDING
Canal and Orchard Streets

Mr. Sandor Jarmulowsky arrived in the Lower East Side in 1870. He

Pushcarts on the Lower East Side, circa 1900.
Courtesy Museum of the City of New York

started out selling rags from a pushcart on Hester Street. He became financially successful and founded a bank for his fellow immigrants in 1873. His bank building was erected in 1895 and was the tallest structure in the neighborhood. The bank's finances stood on shaky grounds. After the Panic of 1907 and the founder's death, the bank finally collapsed. Thousands of immigrant depositors were ruined with the bank's failure. There was no insurance on their deposits.

The building now houses a number of garment factories. Jarmulowsky's name is boldly engraved on the corner façade.

Continue going west along Canal Street to Eldridge Street. Turn right and proceed to...

Stop 78.
HOME OF IRA GERSHWIN
60 Eldridge Street

Ira Gershwin, brother of George Gershwin, was born at this site on December 6, 1896. Ira wrote the lyrics for nearly all of George Gershwin's songs.

Go north on Eldridge Street to...

Stop 79.
FORMER SYNAGOGUE
87 Eldridge Street

This modified tenement building housed two separate congregations in the 1920s; Congregation Tifereth Jeshurun and Congregation Chevrah Anshei Grodno v'Anshei Staputkin.

Proceed to Grand Street and turn right (east)...

Stop 80.
RIDLEY'S DEPARTMENT STORE SITE
Southeast corner Grand & Allen Streets

Ridley's Department Store started as a small shop on this site in 1849. By the 1880s, it had expanded to become the country's largest retail store. The building covered an entire city block, from Orchard to Allen Street (before Allen Street was widened in 1930). Only one third of the original structure is still extant. Ridley's closed in 1901. Another large clothing store, located nearby at Grand Street and Broadway, was the original Lord and Taylor.

Shopping at Ridley's on Grand Street, circa 1890.
Courtesy John Grafton's New York in the 19th Century (Dover)

Continue walking to Essex Street, cross over and turn left.

Stop 81.

BIRTHPLACE OF B'NAI B'RITH
Essex Street, between Grand & Broome

About one hundred and fifty feet from the northeast corner of Grand Street is an historic plaque marking the site of the birthplace of the Jewish organization, *B'nai B'rith*, on October 13, 1843.

They met in Sinsheimer's Cafe, which was once located at 60 Essex Street.

Look across the street at the large school...

Stop 82.

SEWARD PARK HIGH SCHOOL
350 Grand Street

Built in 1929 on the site of the old Ludlow Street Prison, Seward Park High School was named in honor of the Secretary of State, William Seward, who was responsible for the purchase of Alaska from Russia. That purchase was known as "Seward's Folly."

Among the sons of the Lower East Side who graduated from this school are actors Zero Mostel and Walter Matthau.

Double back to Grand Street and turn left (east). Go one block and turn left at Norfolk Street...

Stop 83.

BETH HAMEDRASH HAGADOL
60 Norfolk Street   Tel. (212) 674-3330

Built in 1852 as the Norfolk Street Baptist Church, the Gothic Revival building was purchased in 1885 by the Orthodox Jewish congregation that is still housed in it. It is, therefore, the home of the oldest Orthodox congregation in the city continuously housed in a single location.

In 1899, Rabbi Jacob Joseph from Vilna was appointed rabbi of the congregation. He was later given the short-lived title of "Chief Rabbi" of the City of New York.

Return to Grand Street and turn left. Walk three blocks until you get to...

Stop 84.

CHURCH OF SAINT MARY
440 Grand Street   Tel. (212) 674-3266

The Church of Saint Mary is the oldest Roman Catholic church structure in New York City. It was built in 1832. The brick façade, with its wooden trims and door frames, and the twin spires, are additions dating from 1871, and were designed by the prolific church architect Patrick Charles Keely. The main part of the structure is composed of rough-hewn fieldstone (Manhattan schist), revealing the architectural (Federal) style of the 1830s.

Continue walking east along Grand Street to the next corner...

Stop 85.

HENRY STREET SETTLEMENT PLAYHOUSE
466 Grand Street   Tel. (212) 598-0400

This is a branch of the Henry Street Settlement. It started as a theater for the Settlement's amateur productions but soon became a house for professional theater as well. Graduates of the acting course given here include Gregory Peck, Tammy Grimes, Diane Keaton, Eli Wallach and Lorne Greene.

Walk one block to Willett (Bialystoker) Street, turn left...

Stop 86.

BIALYSTOKER SYNAGOGUE
7 Bialystoker (Willett) Street   Tel. (212) 475-0165

Built in 1826 as the Willett Street Methodist Church, the field-stone structure is an official New York City landmark. Before the Civil War, the building was used as part of the "Underground Railroad" which smuggled black slaves from the South to "safe houses" in the North. There is a secret "trap door" located at the northwest corner on the balcony level. It has been painted over but can be seen if you look carefully.

The Orthodox Congregation Anshei Bialystok, which had been organized on Orchard Street in 1878, purchased this building in 1905. It is the oldest structure in the city to house a synagogue. The lavish Ark with its exquisite gold-leaf details was designed in Italy. There are three sculptural crowns above the Ark as well as two bold lions perched on top.

Since the building has been declared an official city landmark, the exterior façades cannot be altered. This posed a problem when the congre-

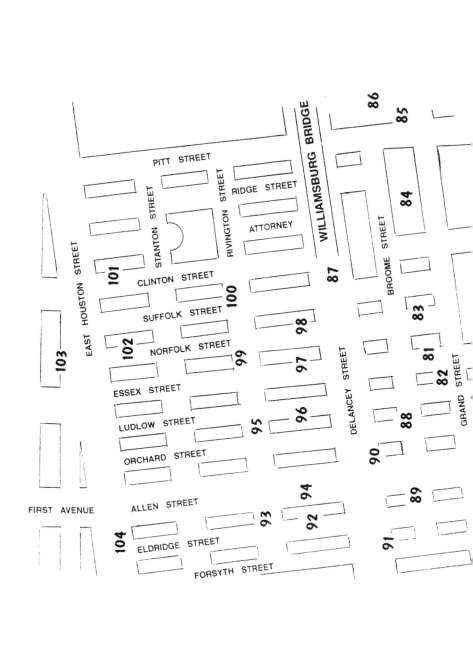

gation wanted to install a central air conditioning unit. It was not permitted to be installed on any exterior part of the building. Two large units were therefore built *inside* the synagogue's upper balcony (east wall) and enclosed with sheetrock partitions.

The Bialystoker Synagogue was recently restored at a cost of over $250,000. The original ceiling and wall murals depicting the signs of the zodiac and scenes of Jerusalem were completely restored to their 1905 elegance.

The unique wash basin in the lobby of the synagogue was originally two oak wine barrels. They were restored and donated by Schapiro's Winery, still located on Rivington Street.

Bialystok was a major Jewish city in Poland/Russia (the borders changed hands after each war) before World War II. Be sure to see the Bialystoker Home for the Aged, located at 228 East Broadway. It is designed in the Art Deco style and has a Jewish mural on its east façade. And, of course, don't forget to buy a "Bialy" (an onion roll originating in Bialystok) at their bakery on Grand Street.

That large bridge above Willett Street is...

Stop 87.

WILLIAMSBURG BRIDGE
East end of Delancey Street

The arrival of hundreds of thousands of East European Jews after 1900 and the razing of entire blocks of Lower East Side tenements to make way for the Williamsburg Bridge approach along Delancey Street in 1903, caused a great surge of Jewish migration over to Williamsburg, Brooklyn, directly across the East River.

The bridge, with its pedestrian ramps, trolley lines and subways, became a major link between the Jewish communities of the Lower East Side, Williamsburg and Brownsville/East New York.

Double back to Grand Street, turn right (west) and continue to Orchard Street. Turn right and walk one block to...

Stop 88.

LOWER EAST SIDE TENEMENT MUSEUM
90 Orchard Street   Tel. (212) 431-0233

"Tenement" is the term used to describe a five- or six-story walk-up apartment building. Many buildings of this style, designed for the masses of immigrants who came to New York City after the 1870s are located in the Lower East Side.

Construction of the Williamsburg Bridge in 1903.
Courtesy Merlis Collection.

There are usually stores on either side of a central (metal) staircase. The entrance foyer is very narrow. A typical residential floor was originally designed to accommodate four small apartments. There were two toilets or water closets in the public corridor. Originally, there were no showers or baths in these "cold water flats." Some lucky immigrants would have a bathtub located in the kitchen, near the building's water lines. They would put a plank of wood over the tub, and voila, they would have a dining area!

Most immigrants, however, would go to the public bathhouses. The last public bathhouse in the Lower East Side was located at 133 Allen Street. That building was recently converted into an Oriental church. Today, all apartments in these old tenement buildings are required by law to have complete built-in bathrooms.

The central core of the tenement was required to have an air shaft. These air shafts often measured about two feet in depth. All rooms which required a window (bedroom, bathroom, etc.) often faced these dingy air shafts. The shape that these air shafts created in plan view, on both sides of each tenement, was a "dumbbell" shape, hence the term,"Dumbbell Tenement."

So now, when you are looking at a continuous row of tenements, there are actually these air spaces (about four feet wide) between each building.

The Lower East Side Tenement Museum is located in a restored 1863 tenement on Orchard Street. The tour of the museum starts at 90 Orchard Street (corner Broome Street), where the visitor sees a short film in a mini-theater about the Lower East Side and its immigrant groups. The tour then proceeds across the street to #97 Orchard Street, where the visitors proceed to climb upstairs and view the restored tenement apartments, complete with turn of the century furniture and artifacts. Note: Group tours can accommodate up to fifteen people. Reservations are recommended.

Diagonally across the street from the Lower East Side Tenement Museum gallery and ticket office (on Broome Street, between Orchard and Allen Streets), is the Lower East Side Tourist Information Center.

Walk west on Broome Street, cross Allen Street and come to...

Stop 89.

GREEK SYNAGOGUE & MUSEUM
280 Broome Street   Tel. (212) 431-1619

The majority of the Jewish immigrants who arrived in the Lower East Side around the turn of the century came from Eastern Europe and were fleeing the pogroms. These were known as the Ashkenazic Jews. There were also several groups who arrived from the Mediterranean countries.

Romaniote
Female Costume

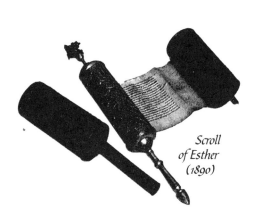

Scroll
of Esther
(1890)

Torah from Janina, Greece

Hand-carved Shofar

They were known as Sephardic Jews.

This small congregation on Broome Street has a magnificent and unique history. They are neither Ashkenazik nor Sephardic. They are Jews who, after the destruction of the Holy Temple in Jerusalem in the year 70 A.C.E., were sent on a slave ship to Rome. Instead, a storm forced them to land in Greece, where over the next two thousand years, they developed uniquely different ethnic and religious customs. This group was called *Romaniotes*.

They settled in the town of Janina. They welcomed the Spanish and Portuguese (Sephardic) Jews after they were expelled from their respective countries during the Inquisition of 1492.

The Kehila Kedosha Janina Synagogue in the Lower East Side is the only synagogue in the Western Hemisphere of this tiny and obscure Greek Jewish community. There are weekly Sabbath services as well as on all Jewish holidays.

Upstairs in the womens' section is a beautiful exhibition of the history of the Jews of Janina, including a Holocaust memorial and the tragic events which wiped out virtually 90% of Greek and Janina Jewry.

The congregation in New York was founded in 1906. The small synagogue is a replica of the one in Janina, Greece and was built in 1927.

The synagogue is open on Sundays from 11:00 am to 4:00 pm or other times by reservation. Admission is by contribution.

Double back to Allen Street, turn left and walk one block to Delancey Street...

Stop 90.

BANK OF THE UNITED STATES SITE
79 Delancey Street

This imposing structure was for many years the Bank of the United States. It was owned mostly by Jews and was believed to be an official institution of the United States Government, hence many of the Jewish immigrants invested their life savings in it. After the stock market crash of 1929, the bank fell upon hard times. When many of the major banks refused to grant the Bank of the United States short-term credit, many immigrants considered anti-Semitism to be the reason. The bank did actually fail in 1932, but most of the depositors were able to salvage most of their savings.

In the 1930s, the building was occupied by the Hebrew Publishing Company until the early 1980s. That company moved out to New Jersey.

Walk west (left) along Delancey Street for two blocks. You have reached the corner of Delancey and Forsyth Streets and...

Stop 91.

UNION SQUARE
SEVENTH DAY ADVENTIST CHURCH
128-130 Forsyth Street

On the southeast corner of Delancey and Forsyth Streets stands the Union Square Seventh Day Adventist Church. It was originally built as a synagogue in 1895 for Congregation Poel Zedek Anshe Ileya. The most fascinating feature in this building is along its Delancey Street façade. At the street level there were stores. These stores actually helped in the upkeep of the synagogue and then the church. In more recent times, there were Jewish shopkeepers in these stores paying rent to the church.

Cross Delancey Street and go one block to Eldridge Street, turn right until you get to...

Stop 92.

UNIVERSITY SETTLEMENT HOUSE
84 Eldridge Street

The University Settlement Society was organized in 1886. It was founded for the purpose of bringing men of education into closer relations with the laboring classes of the city, for mutual instruction and benefit. It aims to establish "settlements" in the tenement-house districts, where college men could carry out, or induce others to "carry out, all the reforms, domestic, industrial, educational, provident, or recreative, which the social ideal demands." The building still houses a community center.

Continue walking north along Eldridge Street. When you get to Rivington Street, turn right (east)...

Stop 93.

FORMER SYNAGOGUE
58 Rivington Street

Congregation Adath Jeshurun of Jassy was organized in 1886 and built in 1903. The congregation later moved out and was replaced by the First Warsaw Congregation. That congregation disbanded as well. Several years ago, the building was purchased by a local artist.

Walk down Rivington Street (eastward) for one block to Allen Street, turn right...

Stop 94.

PUBLIC BATHS (former)
133 Allen Street

The Tenement Reform Bill of April, 1901 prohibited the further construction of the "dumbbell" tenement. According to the new law, every residential building completed after January 1, 1902 had to allow for direct natural lighting of every room and to conform to such minimal health and safety standards as separate toilet facilities for each apartment and safely constructed fire escapes.

The immigrants who, unfortunately, had to live in the "old law" tenements would have to go to public bathhouses such as this one, located at 133 Allen Street, since their buildings did not have any shower or bath facilities.

This building was closed down by city health inspectors several years ago following the upsurge of the AIDS epidemic. Many homeless and "infected" people would come to this facility. It was therefore decided to close down the facility. The building was recently converted into the Church of Grace to Fujanese N.Y.

The last public bath facility in the area has recently been restored. It is located on East 23rd Street, on the corner of Asser Levy Place, near the FDR Drive. Asser Levy was one of the original twenty-three Jews who arrived in New Amsterdam in 1654. The public bath facility was designed in 1906 by Arnold Brunner and William Martin Aiken.

Arnold Brunner was a noted architect who designed the present synagogue building for America's oldest congregation, Shearith Israel, in 1897. He also designed the Educational Alliance in the Lower East Side, Temple Beth El (Fifth Avenue & 76th (Street), the West End Synagogue (166 West 82nd Street) and Temple Israel of Harlem.

Cross Allen Street and proceed east along Rivington Street...

Stop 95.

THE ROUMANIASHE SHUL
89 Rivington Street   Tel. (212) 673-2835

Built as a Methodist church in 1888, the building was purchased just a few years after construction by Congregation Shaarey Shomayim, also known as the First Roumanian-American Congregation, but lovingly known as the *Roumaniashe Shul* by the locals.

The voices of such world-class cantors as Yossele Rosenblatt, Moshe Kousevitzky, Moishe Oysher, Jan Peerce and his brother-in-law, Richard Tucker resounded through the hallowed halls of the 1200 seat synagogue. The Roumaniashe Shul has been called the *Cantors' Carnegie Hall.*

The last public bath house is now an Oriental church.

There are daily services at 8 am and at 5 pm, primarily serving the local merchants, as well as on the Sabbath and the major Jewish holidays. The Romanesque Revival building has just undergone an exterior facelift, showing its original red brick surface. Tours are available by prior arrangements. The small building to the left of the synagogue at No. 95 Orchard Street once housed the congregation's Talmud Torah.

Turn right at Ludlow Street for...

Stop 96.

FORMER SYNAGOGUE
121 Ludlow Street

The main sanctuary of this former synagogue is now used as a warehouse. Chevrah Kadisha Anshei Sochechov was housed in this remodeled tenement in the 1920s.

Double back to Rivington Street, turn right (east) and continue walking to Essex Street...

Stop 97.

ESSEX STREET MARKET
Essex Street, between Broome and Stanton Streets

For many of the newly-arrived immigrants around the turn of the century, the sweatshops were the only places where these unskilled laborers could find jobs. The working conditions were intolerable, not only because of the overcrowding and filth but also because they had to work twelve to sixteen hours a day, seven days a week, including Saturday, the Jewish Sabbath. A sign posted on the wall of the sweatshop stated quite simply, "If you don't come in to work on Saturday, don't bother coming in on Sunday!"

Many immigrants continued to work on the Sabbath since they had no other means of supporting their large families. Others went into business for themselves. They rented pushcarts and made their own "business hours." The streets were filled with these pushcarts, selling everything from rags *(shmat'es)* to buttons and thread. Orchard Street was a major artery for these pushcarts.

In the early 1930s, the city banned all pushcarts from Orchard Street, declaring that they were a major fire hazard–fire trucks could not pass through the pushcart-congested street. At that time, the Essex Street Market was constructed. It was designed to house all of the outlawed pushcarts from Orchard Street.

The Market has, over the years, become dilapidated and run down. Part of the Essex Street Market, near Stanton Street, has recently been converted into a local medical center.

Cross Essex Street and continue eastward on Rivington Street...

Stop 99.

SCHAPIRO'S KOSHER WINERY
124 Rivington Street   Tel. (212) 674-4404

Founded in 1899, Schapiro's Kosher Wines still uses the original oak vats in their cellar. The cellar actually continues under the sidewalks of Rivington Street. Kosher wine means that the processing of the wines are under rabbinical supervision. All of Schapiro's wines are processed in upstate New York and are *mevushal* (cooked), which is another step in the kashruth process.

During the Depression years, Schapiro's was permitted to operate since its product was for sacramental (religious) use.

Tours and wine tasting in the only kosher winery in Manhattan are available on Sundays or by appointment.

Proceed eastward on Rivington Street...

Stop 100.

STREITS MATZOH FACTORY
150 Rivington Street   Tel. (212) 475-7000

The only matzoh factory in Manhattan is located at the corner of Rivington and Suffolk Streets. Tour of the facilities are no longer available due to insurance company restrictions. However, it is possible to purchase fresh products in the small store which carries Streits products. You can look into the factory and still see the modern machinery with conveyer belts carrying consolidated sheets of matzoh before they are broken into squares and packed into boxes.

At Clinton Street, turn left and go north toward Houston Street...

Stop 101.

CONGREGATION CHASAM SOPHER
8 Clinton Street   Tel. (212) 777-5140

This is the second oldest synagogue structure in New York City. It was built in 1853 for Congregation Rodef Shalom. That congregation is still functioning and is located on the Upper West Side at 7 West 83rd Street. Congregation Chasam Sopher purchased the building in 1891. The Orthodox Congregation Chasam Sopher is assisted in its upkeep and

Chasam Sopher' building was designed in 1853.

maintenance by its Reform predecessor, Rodef Shalom. Rodef Shalom feels it still has a link to its roots in the Lower East Side.

Walk back to Houston Street, turn left. At Norfolk Street, turn left...

Stop 102.

OLDEST SYNAGOGUE BUILDING
172 Norfolk Street

Ansche Chesed was organized in 1828 by German Jews. It built this lavish Gothic Revival synagogue in 1849. It was designed by architect Alexander Saeltzer. It had a seating capacity of 1500. In 1874, the first congregation moved out and was replaced by Congregation Ohab Zedek. That second congregation moved to Harlem and is presently located on Manhattan's Upper West Side. The building was taken over in 1921 by Congregation Anshe Slonim. That congregation began to dwindle after World War II.

By 1975, the building stood abandoned and was slated for demolition. However, in 1986 the building was purchased at auction by a Spanish Jewish artist, Angel Orensanz, for $500,000. He now uses the lofty space of the main sanctuary as his studio and gallery.

Walk back to Houston Street, look across the street at a modern residential high-rise...

Stop 103.

RED SQUARE
250 East Houston Street

There is something a little peculiar about this building. Look at that clock on the roof. The numbers are all screwed up. There is also a 18-foot-high copper statue of Nikolai Lenin! There seems to be some connection with the owner of the building and the former Soviet Union...

Walk westward along Houston Street until you get to...

Stop 104.

SUNSHINE THEATER (former)
147 East Houston Street

This building was built ca. 1910 as the Sunshine Theater. There were plans to renovate the building into a cafe and club.

Double back on Houston Street, cross over and go toward Avenue A. Look for a small free-standing little synagogue...

18-foot-high copper statue of Lenin on top of Red Square apartment house was designed in Russia by Peter Gerasimov.

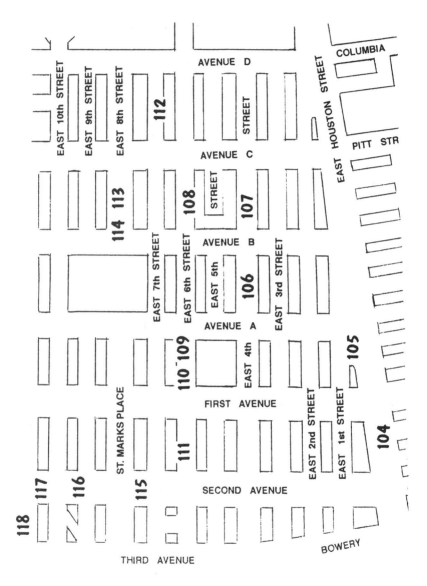

East
Village

Stop 105.

FORMER SYNAGOGUE
108 East 1st Street

Congregation Masas Benjamin Anshe Podhajce was an active congregation until the 1970s. Some young members in the community tried to keep the minyan going as long as they could. But in the late 1980s, the congregation folded. The synagogue had a magnificent bimah reminiscent of a medieval Polish shtetl synagogue.

The building was taken over by a group which held concerts and poetry readings. It was known as "Synagogue Space." In recent years, the building has been turned into residential spaces.

Walk on East Houston Street to Avenue B. Turn left and go north to East 4th Street. Turn right and go to...

Stop 106.

FORMER SYNAGOGUE
256 East 4th Street

Stop 107.

FORMER SYNAGOGUE
289 East 4th Street

This building housed Congregation Nachlath Zvi B'nai Israel Linath Hazedek B'nai Menashe in the 1920s.

Continue walking east to Avenue C. Turn left and go to East 6th Street. If you go to the right you will see...

Stop 108.

FORMER SYNAGOGUE
638 East 6th Street

This was the site of Congregation Ahavath Jeshurun Shaare Torah. The building on the right may have been the congregation's Hebrew school, but both structures look like two individual synagogues.

At Avenue C, if you turn left on East 6th Street, you will come to...

Stop 109.

FORMER SYNAGOGUE
431 East 6th Street

The Center of the Proskurove Zion Congregation has been converted into a residential apartment building.

Stop 110.

CONG. AYDUS YISROEL ANSHEI MEZRICH
415 East 6th Street

This small synagogue, designed in Classic Revival style, was organized in 1892 and built in 1910. It is still functioning.

Stop 111.

COMMUNITY SYNAGOGUE CENTER
325 East 6th Street   Tel. (212) 473-3665

Built in 1848 for the United German Lutheran Church. The church group went on an outing to the Bear Mountains in the late 1930s but met with disaster. The boat which the church group was sailing on capsized, drowning the entire congregation.

In 1940, the Community Synagogue purchased the former church building.

Double back at First Avenue. Turn left and walk one block to East 7th Street. Go past Avenue C to...

Stop 112.

SYNAGOGUE CONDOS
242 East 7th Street

The Beth Hamedrash Hagadol Anshe Ungarin was organized in 1883. The congregation designed this lovely Classic Revival synagogue in 1905. It was recently renovated and turned into condominiums.

Double back to Avenue C, turn right and go to East 8th Street. Turn left and go west to...

Stop 113.

EIGHTH STREET SYNAGOGUE
317 East 8th Street   Tel. (212) 529-7557

This building once housed two separate congregations—B'nai Moses Joseph and Chevra Lecheth Yosher B'nai Horowitz. In recent years, the building was literally falling apart. Several local Jews are now in the

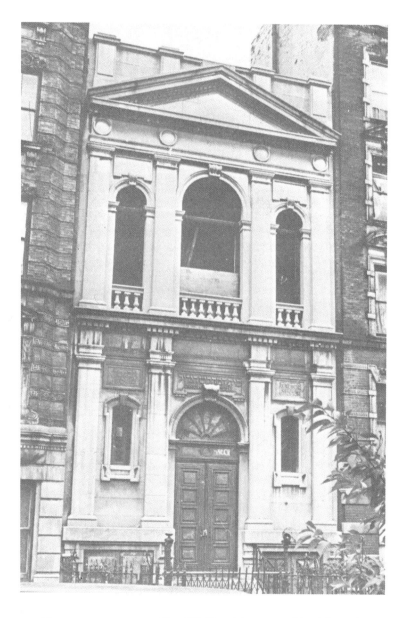

Former synagogue on East 7th Street is now residential condos.

process of stabilizing and restoring the old shul. The congregation is now called the Eighth Street Shul. There are special educational programs and concerts presented by the small community-oriented congregation.

Stop 114.

EAST SIDE HEBREW INSTITUTE (former)
Avenue B and East 8th Street

This was one of several major Hebrew schools or yeshivas in the Lower East Side. It was built before World War I. In the 1960s, this area was in decline. It was known as "Alphabet City" (named so because of the street names—Avenue A, B, C, and D). Tompkins Square Park was the site of one of the city's major drug trafficking areas.

In recent years, however, things were improved. The police cleared the park of the drug addicts, the old bombed-out former tenement buildings were torn down or renovated and new "in-fill" housing was constructed. There are now outdoor cafes opposite the park.

The former East Side Hebrew Institute building was abandoned for many years but has also been renovated. There are now residential apartments in the old building. The original name entablature, *Talmud Torah Darchei Noam*, is still visible above the main entrance. It was organized in 1916 and built in 1926.

Walk west to Second Avenue...

Stop 115.

YIDDISH THEATER DISTRICT
Second Avenue—from East 4th to East 12th Streets

Second Avenue was once the "Jewish Rialto" of the Yiddish Theater. Classic plays as well as special productions were presented in Yiddish, the *Mother Tongue* of the majority of the Jewish immigrants who came to America around the turn of the century. They longed for the *Old Country* and many of these plays featured tales of life in the shtetls.

Among the remaining Yiddish theater buildings still standing are the Yiddish Art Theater, once known as the Eden Theater (now the Enter Media Theater) at East 12th Street; the Anderson Yiddish Theater at East 4th Street (now abandoned); and the Orpheum, at St. Marks Place.

At the corner of Second Avenue and East 10th Street is...

Stop 116.

YIDDISH THEATER STARS' WALK
156 Second Avenue

In front of the Second Avenue Deli is the Jewish version of Growmen's Chinese Theater with its Hollywood star-studded sidewalk. Some of the stars along Second Avenue include Molly Picon, Ben Bonus and the Barry Sisters. The sign in front of the deli reads, "This star-studded sidewalk was created to immortalize the great actors, actresses and musicians who graced the stages of the eight Yiddish theaters that once flourished along Second Avenue." There is another sign in the window of the deli which states, "The French have Cassoulet, we have Cholent."

The Second Avenue Deli serves kosher meats but is open seven days a week. A few years ago, Abe Lebewohl, the owner of the Second Avenue Deli, who was loved by everyone in the neighborhood, was gunned down while depositing the days' receipts in the bank.

Diagonally across the street from the Second Avenue Deli is...

Stop 117.

HOME OF PETER STUYVESANT
Second Avenue and East 10th Street

Peter Stuyvesant's mansion once stood on the site of St. Mark's-in-the-Bowery Church. Stuyvesant was the notoriously anti-Semitic Governor of New Amsterdam who greeted the first Jewish settlers in 1654. He put them in jail until orders were received from headquarters of the Dutch West India Company in Amsterdam, Holland. Many of the shareholders in that company were Jewish. They applied pressure on Peter Stuyvesant who ultimately permitted the 23 Jewish immigrants to live freely in the colony on the provision that they not be a "burden on the society."

The graveyard, containing Stuyvesant's vault, is now remodeled in undulating cobblestones and is used as a playground.

Walk down the angled street of East 10th Street, between Second and Third Avenues and look for...

Stop 118.

HEBREW TECHNICAL SCHOOL SITE
26-36 East 10th Street

Founded in 1884, the Hebrew Technical School was a non-sectarian school. It was one of the first technical high schools in the United States. Its last graduating class was in 1939.

The school was conceived at a meeting of the United Hebrew Charities, the Hebrew Orphan Asylum and the Hebrew Free School Association for the purpose of training youths of immigrants in industrial arts. The building has been declared an official historic landmark and is presently part

Greenwich Village

of New York University.

Cross over Astor Place and see a modern replica of an original 1904 subway kiosk. Go past Cooper Union School of Architecture-that mas - sive brownstone structure, and turn left onto Lafayette Street...

Stop 119.

JOSEPH PAPP'S PUBLIC THEATER
425 Lafayette Street   Tel. (212) 598-7100

The Hebrew Immigrant Aid Society (HIAS) was organized in the 1880s and furnished lawyers and interpreters to help the Jewish immigrants through the red tape of Ellis Island Immigration Station. They provided kosher food for steerage passengers who had not eaten any cooked meals since leaving the shtetls in the *Old Country*. They also provided temporary housing and employment information.

The HIAS headquarters was located in this building. It was originally built in 1853 as the Astor Library. It was designed by Alexander Saeltzer (architect of New York City's oldest synagogue structure, Ansche Chesed, located at 172 Norfolk Street, in the Lower East Side). The Astor Library later became part of today's New York Public Library at Fifth Avenue and 42nd Street.

In the late 1960s, the Romanesque Revival building was converted into seven indoor theaters for Joseph Papp's New York Shakespeare Festival. The complex was designed by Giorgio Cavaglieri. The first performance of the great rock musical *Hair* opened in this theater. *A Chorus Line* was also first premiered in this theater. During the summer months, the New York Shakespeare Festival offers free productions in its Central Park theatre-in-the round (near 81st Street). The Joseph Papp's Public Theater has been declared a National Historic Landmark.

Walk south to East 4th Street. Turn right and walk to Broadway...

Stop 120.

HEBREW UNION COLLEGE
One West 4th Street   Tel. (212) 674-5300

In 1922, Stephen S. Wise founded the Jewish Institute of Religion in New York to provide training "for the Jewish ministry, research, and community service." Rabbi Wise was its president until 1948. The school was located adjacent to his Free Synagogue at 30 West 68th Street, in the Upper West Side until its present building was completed in 1980. The Jewish Institute of Religion merged with the Hebrew Institute of Religion (whose main campus is in Cincinnati, Ohio) in 1950.

The College prepares its students for the pulpit in congregations belonging to the Reform Movement. The Hebrew Union College presents lecture programs and museum exhibitions which are open to the general public.

Continue walking west along West 4th Street to Greene Street. Turn right and go to Washington Place...

Stop 121.

TRIANGLE FIRE SITE
Washington Place & Greene Street

A bronze plaque at the northwest corner of Washington Place and Greene Street (just east of Washington Square Park in Greenwich Village) refers to the site of the Triangle Shirtwaist Company fire, a tragedy which took 143 lives, mostly young women, on the Saturday afternoon of March 25, 1911. The Loft Building which stands today on this corner, originally called the Asch Building, is the very building in which that holocaust took place.

The Triangle Company occupied the upper three floors of the ten-story structure. The owner of that sweatshop refused to let his workers go for coffee breaks, so he locked the doors to the factory—from the outside. When fire did break out, the young women couldn't open the exit doors and were forced to jump out the windows!

Following the fire, new and more stringent child-labor laws were instituted. State legislation provided for factory fire prevention and building inspection, sanitary working conditions, workmen's compensation and liability insurance, and shortened hours of labor for women and children.

This building is part of the New York University campus.

Walk into Washington Square Park, which once had public hangings...

Stop 122.

WASHINGTON ARCH

This beautiful arch was originally designed by McKim, Mead & White in wood in 1876 in honor of America's Centennial. It was later rebuilt (1892) by the same architects in white marble.

Walk north along Fifth Avenue to 16th Street. Turn left to see...

Stop 123.

CENTER FOR JEWISH HISTORY
15 West 16th Street (under construction)

Triangle Fire of March 25, 1911.

The Ultimate Judaica Store

BOOKS JUDAICA

J. LEVINE CO.

SINCE 1890

ULTIMATE LOCATION

Blocks from the Empire State Building, Macy's, A&S, Toys R Us, Penn Station and a multitude of kosher restaurants!

ULTIMATE GIFTS

ULTIMATE NAME

ULTIMATE SELECTION

- books
- seforim
- children's toys
- books & games
- texts
- educational material
- needlepoint kits
- ketubot
- yarmulkes
- tallaism
- tallis bags
- invitations

- challah covers
- matzah covers
- chuppah rentals
- Bar/Batmitzvah Sets
- gift certificates
- haggadahs
- cookbooks
- seder plates
- mezuzahs
- tefillin
- menorahs

- kiddush cups
- candlesticks
- havdalah sets
- jewelry
- art
- videos
- cassettes/CDs
- candy & caris
- torah mantles
- synagogue furniture
- wedding needs
- simcha registry
- and more

ULTIMATE CONVENIENCE

 MasterCard AMERICAN EXPRESS VISA DISCOVER

Phone or fax in your orders!

Phone: (212) 695-6888
Fax: (212) 643-1044

GIFT CERTIFICATES

ULTIMATE SCHEDULE

We're open
Sun. 10-5
(Except July)

Mon. to Wed. 9-6
Thurs. til 7
Fri. til 2

When in Midtown Manhattan
Visit the World's Oldest & Best Judaica Store

J. LEVINE BOOKS & JUDAICA

5 West 30th Street New York, NY 10001

between Fifth Avenue & Broadway

**Present this Ad for a 10% Discount.
Mention this Ad and receive a Free Copy
($10 Value) of our 100-page Catalog.**

TOLL FREE: 1 (800) 5 JEWISH

In NYC (212) 695-6888 • Web Site: www.levine-judaica.com
E-MAIL: sales@levine-judaica.com

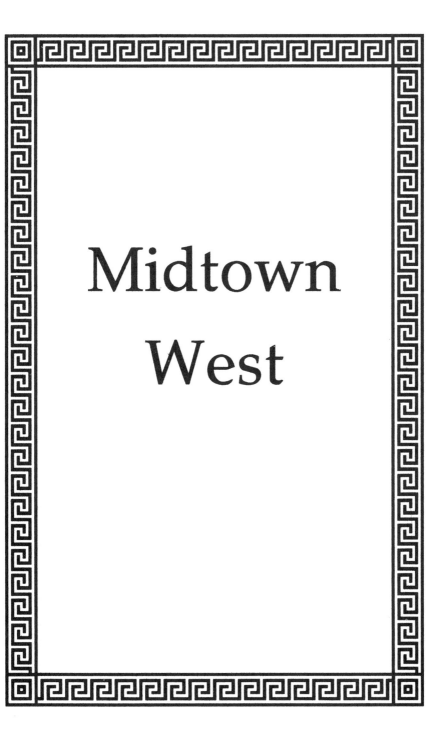

Midtown West

In the spring of 1999, a five-building complex called the Center for Jewish History will open just west of Union Square, bringing together the collections of four of the country's leading authorities on Jewish history: The **American Jewish Historical Society** was founded in 1892 and is presently housed in Brandeis University in Waltham, MA. More than 40 million archival documents and 30,000 books dating from the proceedings against the Jews during the Mexican Inquisition in the 16th century. The **Leo Baeck Institute** was founded in 1955 and is located at 129 East 73rd Street. Sixty-thousand books covering almost every Jewish community in Germany and other areas; periodicals, letters, documents and 1,000 memoirs going back several centuries, and 30,000 photographs.

Yeshiva University Museum was founded in 1973 and is located at the main campus of Yeshiva University in Washington Heights–Amsterdam Avenue and 186th Street. The museum contains architectural models of historic synagogues from Poland, Morocco, Iraq and elsewhere, and a renowned collection of Judaica objects confiscated by the Nazis and rescued by the Jewish Reconstruction Agency.

YIVO Institute was founded in 1925 and was located in a town palace once owned by Mrs. Cornelius Vanderbilt–at Fifth Avenue and 86th Street. YIVO has more than 22 million documents, 350,000 volumes and 200,000 photographs on the civilization of Eastern European Jewry before the Holocaust.

The Center for Jewish History will house and make accessible the most massive Jewish archival collection in the diaspora–100 million documents, original manuscripts and photographs, a library in excess of 500,000 volumes, and more than 10,000 artifacts and works of art. It is the future "Smithsonian of Jewish Studies" and the "Jewish Library of Congress."

At this point, the tour splits in two directions–the Upper West Side and the Upper East Side.
Continue walking west on 16th Street until you reach Sixth Avenue, also known as the Avenue of the Americas. You can walk either right or left to the next sights.

Stops 124. & 125.

HISTORIC JEWISH CEMETERIES
Sixth Avenue–at 11th Street & at 21st Street

There are three historic Jewish cemeteries which belong to America's oldest congregation, Shearith Israel–The Spanish and Portuguese Synagogue–organized in 1654. The first one is located at Chatham Square in Chinatown (Stop 46.). The second *beth haim* (cemetery) is located on West 11th Street, just east of Sixth Avenue (Avenue of the Americas). It was consecrated on February 27, 1805. Shortly after the

Mordecai Manuel Noah was one of the founders of NYU.

yellow fever scourge of 1822, it became the only Jewish cemetery in New York that could be used. Among the few buried in this cemetery is the American soldier and patriot, Ephraim Hart, who was one of the founders of the New York Stock Exchange.

The *beth haim shlishi* or third Jewish cemetery of Congregation Shearith Israel, is located on 21st Street, just west of Sixth Avenue. It was consecrated on August 17, 1829 and was in use for twenty two years. One of the last to be buried here was Mordecai Manuel Noah.

Mordecai Manuel Noah was a well-known politician, playwright, journalist and leader in the Jewish community in New York City. He was named consul to Tunis and was appointed sheriff of New York. He was the principal speaker at the dedication of Shearith Israel's second building in 1818. He was a founder of New York's second oldest congregation, B'nai Jeshurun and was one of the founders of New York University.

The most unique project Mordecai Manuel Noah attempted to create was the Ararat Colony on Grand Island, near Niagara Falls. It was organized in 1825 as a refuge for Jews from all parts of the world. They were to study agriculture, so that when they return to Palestine, they would be able to build up the land. He was the first political Zionist. The grand plans ended in a fiasco. All that remains, however, is a cornerstone engraved with Hebrew and English phrases on Ohio limestone. It can still be viewed in the City Hall on Grand Island (on the ground floor). It has an inscription of the Hebrew prayer, *Shema Yisrael...*

Walk up Sixth Avenue to 34th Street, Herald Square.

Stop 126.

MACY'S DEPARTMENT STORE

Macy's Department Store was the site of Congregation B'nai Jeshurun's third location. B'nai Jeshurun is New York City's second oldest congregation (after the Spanish & Portuguese Synagogue) and first Ashkenazic congregation. It was organized in 1825.

Macy's Department Store was founded by Isador Straus. Isador and his wife Judith Straus died in the sinking of the S.S. Titanic's maiden voyage on April 15, 1912.

Walk to Seventh Avenue, turn right and go to 39th Street.

Stop 127.

GARMENT CENTER MONUMENT

The sculpture designed by Judith Weller in 1984 depicts a garment worker bent over his sewing machine. The figure is wearing a yarmulka (Jewish head covering). It is located in the plaza in front of 555 Seventh Avenue, near 39th Street.

Walk to 47th Street, turn left and go to...

Stop 128.

THE ACTOR'S TEMPLE
339 West 47th Street   Tel. (212) 245-6975

Congregation Ezrat Israel is located in an area known as Hell's Kitchen. It is not too far from the heart of the Theater District. Many Broadway, movie and television stars attend services in this synagogue, known as the Actor's Temple. The lobby contains several caricatures of some of the Jewish-actor-members of the congregation.

Walk back to Seventh Avenue, turn left and go to 57th Street.

Stop 129.

CARNEGIE HALL
881 Seventh Avenue   Tel. (212) 247-7800

The world-class concert hall was built in 1891 by William Morris Hunt. It was threatened with demolition in the 1960s after Lincoln Center for the Performing Arts was completed. Carnegie Hall was rescued by the noted Jewish violinist, Isaac Stern and friends. It was recently restored to its original grandeur. It is an official New York City landmark. Tours of Carnegie Hall are available.

Walk over to Broadway, turn right and walk to 65th Street.

Stop 130.

LINCOLN CENTER FOR THE PERFORMING ARTS

Lincoln Center for the Performing Arts at one time was a run-down neighborhood with four-story tenements. The area was condemned as part of the Lincoln Square Urban Renewal Area in the late 1950s. However, before the buildings were demolished, the site was used in the filming of Leonard Bernstein's musical *West Side Story.*

Lincoln Center for the Performing Arts consists of the Metropolitan Opera House, the New York State Theater, Avery Fisher (Philharmonic) Hall, Vivian Beaumont Theater, Museum of the Performing Arts and the Julliard School of Music.

METROPOLITAN OPERA HOUSE

The grand lobby of the Metropolitan Opera House contains two magnificent paintings by the noted Jewish artist, Marc Chagall. The 30 by 30 foot paintings are titled, *Triumph of Music* and *Sources of Music.* Backstage tours of the Met are available by calling (212) 582-3512.

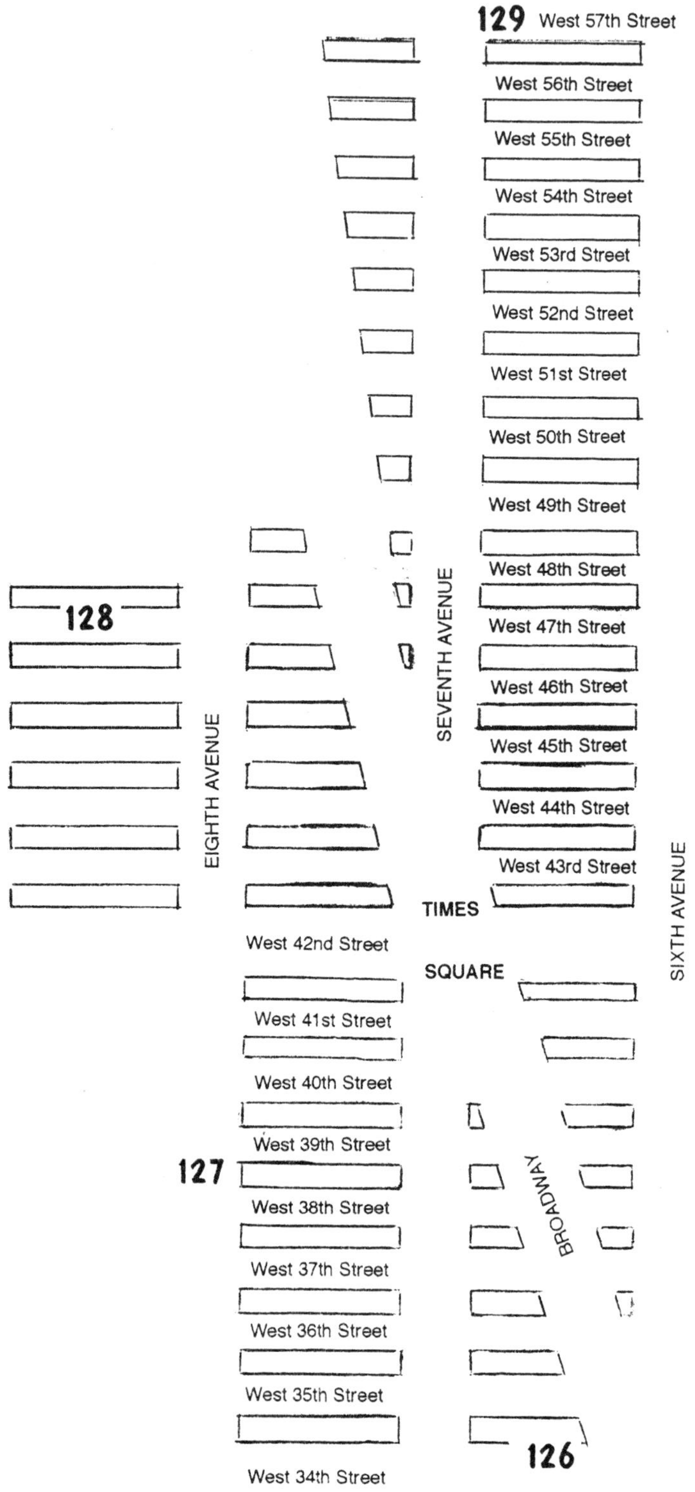

129 West 57th Street

West 56th Street

West 55th Street

West 54th Street

West 53rd Street

West 52nd Street

West 51st Street

West 50th Street

West 49th Street

West 48th Street

West 47th Street

West 46th Street

West 45th Street

West 44th Street

West 43rd Street

SEVENTH AVENUE

SIXTH AVENUE

EIGHTH AVENUE

128

TIMES

SQUARE

West 42nd Street

West 41st Street

West 40th Street

West 39th Street

127

West 38th Street

West 37th Street

West 36th Street

BROADWAY

West 35th Street

126

West 34th Street

Upper
West Side

Across the street from Lincoln Center for the Performing Arts, in a small traffic-island park at Broadway & 66th Street, is...

Stop 131.

RICHARD TUCKER MEMORIAL PARK

Richard Tucker was known as the *Sweet Singer of Israel.* He worked his way up from being a furrier and part-time cantor in the Lower East Side, Crown Heights and the Grand Concourse in the Bronx to the status of being one of the world's greatest operatic tenors. He died of a heart attack while on an operatic tour in 1975. His funeral was held in the Metropolitan Opera House at Lincoln Center.

Continue up Broadway to 66th Street, turn right and proceed to...

Stop 132.

HOLOCAUST SURVIVORS' SYNAGOGUE
44 West 66th Street   Tel. (212) 787-5347

On November 9, 1938, Hitler ordered all of the synagogues in Germany to be destroyed. That was the *Kristallnacht* and marked the beginning of the destruction of of the Jewish communities throughout Europe.

Congregation Habonim was founded in 1939 by a group of refugees from Nazi Germany. There is a small display area in the lobby featuring stone fragments from the Essen Synagogue and the Fassanenstrasse Temple (in Berlin) as well as part of a burned Torah parchment. Congregation followed the Reform ritual until 1997, at which time the congregation adopted the Conservative ritual.

Double back to Broadway, walk to 67th street to...

Stop 133.

HEBREW ARTS SCHOOL
129 West 67th Street   Tel. (212) 362-8060

Founded in 1952, the Hebrew Arts School is a nonprofit, nonsectarian institution dedicated to high-quality instruction in music, dance, art and theater for children and adults. It moved into its own modern building one block north of Lincoln Center for the Performing Arts in 1978.

The Abraham Goodman House, which also contains the famed Merkin Concert Hall, provides the students with the finest facilities for study and performance. There are spacious classrooms, well-equipped instrumental, dance and art studios, the Ann Goodman Recital Hall, an art gallery, music library and recording studio.

Remnants of the destroyed Berlin synagogue on Fasanenstrasse are found in the Habonim Synagogue lobby.

B'nei Jeshurun was organized in 1825.

Highlights of the varied concert series at Merkin Concert Hall include Heritage Concerts, Twilight Concerts of Jewish Music, the American Jewish Choral Festival, the Musica Camerit, and the annual *Judas Maccabeas* Open Sing. The building is closed on the Sabbath and all Jewish holidays.

Doubleback and walk to Columbus Avenue. Turn left and go to 70th Street, turn right and proceed to...

Stop 134.

OLDEST CONGREGATION IN NORTH AMERICA
8 West 70th Street   Tel. (212) 873-0300

Congregation Shearith Israel was organized by twenty three Jewish castaways who landed in New Amsterdam in September, 1654. They did not build their first synagogue on Mill Street until 1730. The congregation moved several times (Crosby Street, West 19th Street and West 70th Street) following the growth of the city's residential neighborhoods. The present building was built in 1897 by Arnold Brunner. It contains a replica of the very first Mill Street Synagogue. This *Little Synagogue* measures 30 by 30 feet and contains original furnishings from the congregation's earlier buildings. This space is used as a daily chapel and for small weddings.

The main sanctuary, which is used only on the Sabbath and on major holidays, contains a magnificent Ark (heychal) made out of marbles from Italy. The reading platform (taybah) contains the original wooden floorboards from the 1730 Mill Street Synagogue. All of the stained-glass windows in the main sanctuary and in the *Little Synagogue* were designed by Louis Comfort Tiffany. They are all in the process of being releaded and restored. The congregation follows the Western Sephardic ritual and is Orthodox. The congregation is also known as the Spanish & Portuguese Synagogue.

Special services for visitors include the holidays of Tisha B'av and Hoshana Rabba. Tours of this landmark synagogue are available by prior arrangements.

Walk north along Central Park West to 76th Street.

Stop 135.

NEW-YORK HISTORICAL SOCIETY
170 Central Park West   Tel. (212) 873-3400

The galleries contain wall-to-wall silver objects, rare maps, antique toys, watercolors by John James Audobon and landscapes by members of the Hudson River School. The library on the second floor is one of the

The Spanish & Portuguese Synagogue was organized in 1654.

major reference libraries of American history.

The New-York Historical Society was used by the Jewish Museum as its temporary home while they were rebuilding and expanding their Fifth Avenue building in 1996.

The large block along 77th at Central Park West is used on the eve of Thanksgiving by Macy's. They inflate the magnificent balloons for their Thanksgiving Day Parade. Cross 77th Street and go to...

Stop 136.

AMERICAN MUSEUM OF NATURAL HISTORY
Central Park West, between 77th & 81st Streets   Tel. (212) 769-5100

The American Museum of Natural History contains more than 34 million specimens and artifacts of gems, minerals, dinosaurs, reptiles, amphibians and sea-shells. Be sure to see the 90-foot fiberglass blue whale in the Hall of Ocean Life, the Star of India sapphire and a cross-section of a 1300-year-old sequoia. There are "hands-on" exhibits in the Discovery Room and continuous films on natural, scientific and anthropological subjects in the Naturmax Theater.

There is a permanent exhibition display of Jewish interest in the Asian Peoples section on the second floor of the museum. The display features information about the history of Asian Jewish communities in Turkey, India, Yemen, Iraq and Iran. There are Jewish ceremonial and folk art objects from the 6th through the 19th century including a silver Torah case designed in the Sephardic tradition.

Walk to 88th Street, turn left and proceed to...

Stop 137.

OLDEST ASHKENAZIC CONGREGATION
257 West 88th Street   Tel. (212) 787-7600

Congregation B'nai Jeshurun was organized as a breakaway from the Spanish & Portuguese Synagogue, America's first congregation. There was only one congregation in New York from 1654 to 1825. In the early 1800s, many Jews from Germany and Poland (Ashkenazic Jews) had enough followers to secede from the "Mother" congregation. This location is the congregation's fifth since its first building, which was purchased on Elm Street from the First Coloured Presbyterian Church.

Today's building was designed in 1918 by architects Herts and Schneider in the Moorish Revival style. Several years ago part of the elaborate stalagtite-like ceiling fell onto the bimah area. Luckily, it happened when nobody was around. The roof was ultimately repaired and the fixed pews were replaced with movable chairs-an open floor plan.

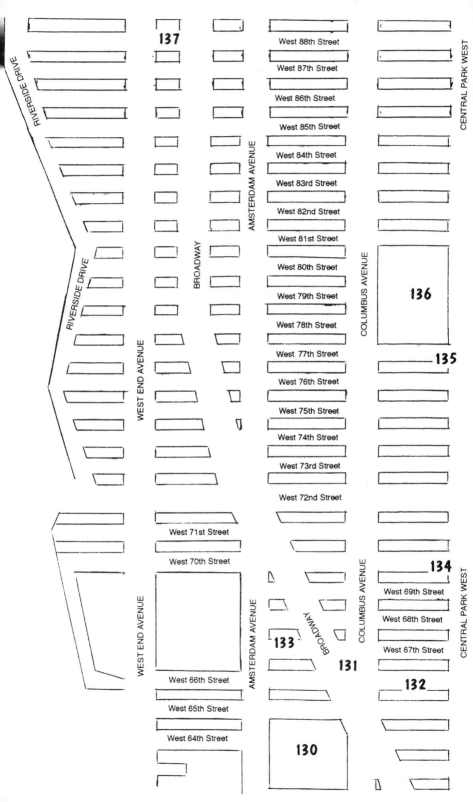

During the restoration of the old building, the congregation has been using a nearby church building, located at 86th Street and West End Avenue, for its Shabbat services. It is a major "singles' scene" on Friday evenings and is known as BJs. The congregation follows the Conservative ritual.

Other single's congregations for followers of the Orthodox tradition are held at Lincoln Square Synagogue (Amsterdam Avenue at 69th Street) and at Ohab Zedek (O.Z.), located on West 95th Street, near Amsterdam Avenue.

Continue north along Broadway to 122nd Street...

Stop 138.

JEWISH THEOLOGICAL SEMINARY
3080 Broadway   Tel. (212) 678-8000

This is where Conservative rabbis receive their training on the East Coast. In 1966, a fire in the old library tower destroyed many thousands of rare manuscripts and books, including some of the fragments discovered by Solomon Schechter in the Cairo *Geniza*. In 1983, a new fireproof library and exhibit hall was constructed on the east wing of the Seminary complex. It was designed by Gruzen and Partners. A series of architectural terraces and arcades were designed to blend-in with the existing structures. The first floor of the new library wing contains changing exhibitions relating to Jewish history. The Jewish Museum is under the auspices of the Jewish Theological Seminary.

We now return to the Midtown and Upper East Side section of the tour...
Start at Madison Square Park, Madison Avenue at 25th Street

Stop 139.

HOLOCAUST MEMORIAL

Along the north end of the Madison Avenue side of the New York State Supreme Court (Appelate Division) is a white marble monumental shaft depicting a map of Auschwitz Concentration Camp.

Walk to First Avenue and 46th Street...

Stop 140.

UNITED NATIONS HEADQUARTERS

The United Nations was designed by an international committee of twelve architects that included Le Corbusier, Oscar Niemeyer and Sven

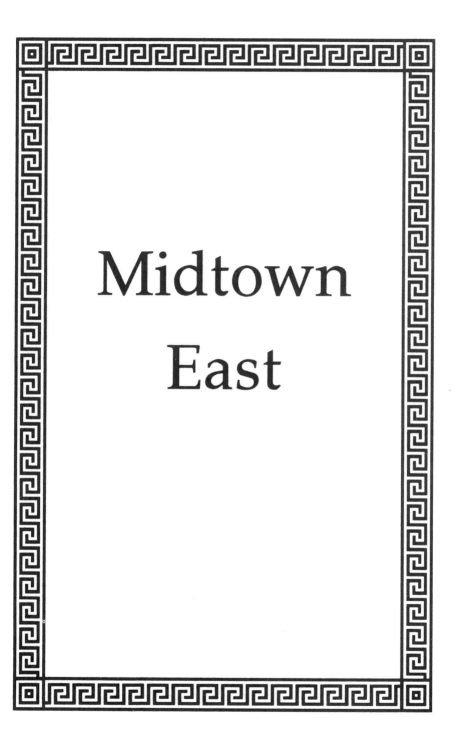

Midtown

East

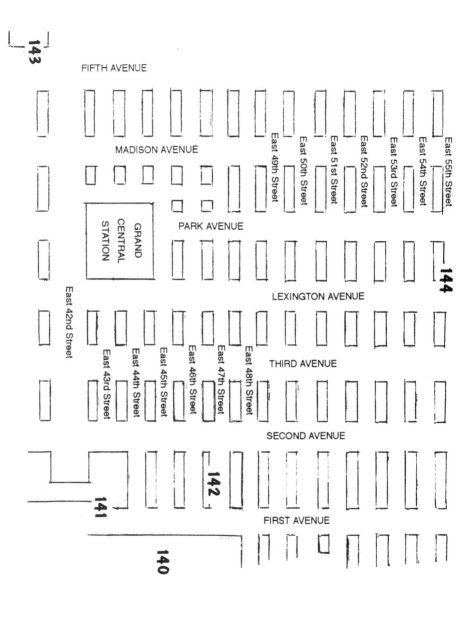

Markelius but headed by the American firm of Harrison, Abramovitz & Harris. The thirty-nine-story Secretariat Building was New York City's first building with all-glass walls which are suspended between 72-foot-wide slabs of Vermont marble.

The flags of member nations fly in alphabetical order along First Avenue. Every major nation has donated some work of art to the United Nations Headquarters. Be sure to see the Marc Chagall stained-glass windows in the lobby of the General Assembly Building. For tour information call (212) 963-4440.

Across the street from the United Nations,
by the set of staircases going up to Tudor City is...

Stop 141.

ISAIAH WALL

Located directly opposite the United Nations Headquarters is this massive granite monument with the words of the prophet Isaiah inscribed on its face, *They shall beat their swords into plowshears and their spears into pruning hooks. Nation shall not lift up sword against nation, neither shall they learn war any more.*

The stairs ascending up to Tudor City were named in honor of the Soviet dissident, Natan Scharansky (who now holds a prominent position is Israel's governing party).

Walk to 47th Street and First Avenue, turn left and look on south wall...

Stop 142.

HOLOCAUST MEMORIALS

On the south side of this large block, known as Dag Hammarskjold Plaza, along the side wall of the B'nai B'rith International headquarters, are seven bronze plaques designed in memory to the six million Jewish men, women and children who perished during the Holocaust. The sculptural plaques were designed by Arbit Blatas in 1980.

There are similar Holocaust memorials designed by this artist in Paris (in the Memorial to the Unknown Jewish Martyr at 17, rue Geoffroy-l'Asnier) and in the Venice Ghetto, next to the Jewish Rest Home.

Walk to Fifth Avenue, turn left and proceed to 42nd Street...

Stop 143.

NEW YORK PUBLIC LIBRARY
Fifth Avenue & 42nd Street   Tel. (212) 930-0800

The New York Public Library houses a research library that contains more than six million books and 17 million documents, including 21 specialized collections of American history, art, periodicals and Slavic, Jewish and Oriental literature. There are four floors of stacks beneath the building and under Bryant Park.

Some of the library's changing exhibits in the Gottesman Exhibition Hall included the Dead Sea Scrolls and medieval Judaica, including works from the Vatican archives.

The Jewish Division of the New York Public Library started in November 1897, when Jacob H. Schiff, the noted philanthropist, donated $10,000 for the purchase of Semitic literature. The Jewish Division started as a reference library for scholars. It became a multi-service, multi-level archive used by people from all over the world. It contains more than 140,000 volumes dealing with Jewish subjects, including medieval and modern literature, Talmudic and midrashic writings, and commentaries. The Jewish Division has one of the largest collections of Jewish periodicals ever assembled in this country.

Doubleback and walk to 55th Street, turn right and go to the corner of Lexington Avenue.

Stop 144.

CENTRAL SYNAGOGUE
123 East 55th Street   Tel. (212) 838-5122

The Central Synagogue was designed in the Moorish Revival style in 1872 by Henry Fernbach, the first Jewish architect in America. His design was inspired by the Great Dohany utca Synagogue in Budapest, Hungary . The Central Synagogue was organized in the Lower East Side by Bohemian Jews in 1839. When Congregation Shaaray Hashomayim merged wither another congregation, Ahavath Chesed, they created the Central Synagogue in 1872.

The Central Synagogue has been declared an official New York City, New York State and National Historic Landmark. It is the oldest synagogue building in continuous use by only one congregation. The cornerstone of the Central Synagogue was laid in 1870 by Rabbi Isaac Mayer Wise, whose son later became rabbi of the congregation. The Central Synagogue follows the Reform ritual.

The synagogue's community house, located across the street at 123 East 55th Street, is home to the Folksbeine Playhouse which presents Yiddish theater productions.

Walk along Lexington Avenue. Go past Bloomingdale's to East 65th Street. Turn left and go to No. 1.

The Central Synagogue was built in 1872.
Courtesy Merlis Collection

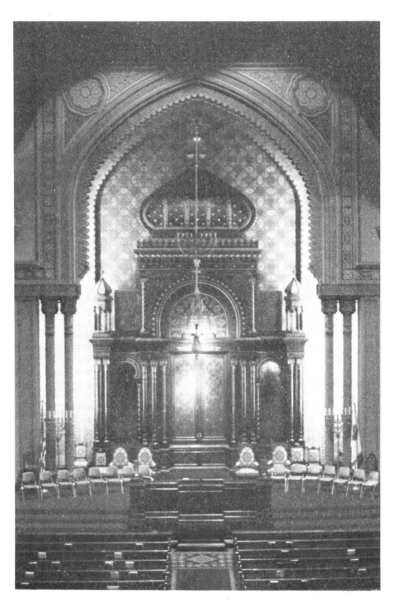

Interior of the Central Synagogue.

Upper
East Side

Interior of Temple Emanu-El.
Courtesy American Jewish Archives

Stop 145.

LARGEST REFORM TEMPLE IN THE WORLD
One East 65th Street   Tel. (212) 744-1400

Temple Emanu-El is the largest Reform congregation in the world, with over 3400 family members. It was organized by German Jews in the Lower East Side in a small room of a tenement, as a *shteebl*, in 1845. The present building (the congregation's fifth location) was built on the site of the old Vincent Astor mansion. It was designed by Robert D. Kohn, Charles Butler and Clarence Stein; with Mayers, Murray & Philip, consultants.

The main body of the auditorium which seats 2,500 is 77 feet wide, 150 feet in length and 103 feet high. The walls of the building are actually bearing or self supporting. The exposed ceiling timbers are reminiscent of the El Transito Synagogue in Toledo, Spain (built in 1357).

The rose window, Gothic in design, is located above the main entrance on Fith Avenue. The twelve petals are symbolic of the twelve tribes of Israel. The stained-glass was designed in England.

There are six stained-glass windows in the main auditorium which depict historic synagogues. The former temple building which was built in 1868 on Fifth Avenue and 43rd Street, and the former Temple Beth El which was located at Fifth Avenue and 76th Street, are portrayed in a window located at the southwest corner of the auditorium. That same wall has stain-glass windows portraying the congregation's first and second buildings (located at Chrystie Street and at East 12th Street, near fourth Avenue) as well. On the opposite wall (at the northeast corner of the auditorium-near the Ark) are portrayals of the Alt-Nue Synagogue in Prague, Slovakia, and the Rashi Shul, located in Worms, Germany. Each of these images is located about 15 feet above the auditorium floor.

The Beth El Chapel adjoins the main auditorium. It is named after Temple Beth El which merged with Temple Emanu-El in 1927. This exquisite chapel is designed in the Byzantine motif and is used for small weddings and Bar or Bat Mitvahs. The two domes of the chapel are supported by six columns of pink Westerly granite, while the side walls rest on arches springing from columns of Breche Oriental marble. Verdello marble is used for the wainscots. the stained-glass windows above the Ark, depicting scenes of Jerusalem and its Holy Temple, were designed by Louis Comfort Tiffany and were removed from the former Temple Emanu-El building located at Fifth Avenue and 43rd Street.

There are only thin curtains separating the main sanctuary from the Beth El Chapel. They are used only one at a time. If there is a service in the main sanctuary, nothing is scheduled for the chapel and vice-versa.

The Herbert & Eileen Bernard Museum of Congregation Emanu-El of New York is located on the second floor of the Community House. The congregation's history offers a significant view of the acculturation of the

Temple Emanu-El is located on Fifth Avenue & 65th Street
Courtesy Merlis Collection

East 83rd Street

East 82nd Street

East 81st Street

East 80th Street

East 79th Street

East 78th Street

147

East 77th Street

East 76th Street

East 75th Street

East 74th Street

East 73rd Street

East 72nd Street

East 71st Street

East 70th Street

East 69th Street

East 68th Street

146

East 67th Street

East 66th Street

145

East 65th Street

FIFTH AVENUE

MADISON AVENUE

PARK AVENUE

LEXINGTON AVENUE

THIRD AVENUE

Jewish people to American society. However, the treasures housed in the Bernard Museum reflect both an older and larger Jewish experience; its material has been collected from Jewish communities throughout the United States, Europe, North Africa and the Near East. These precious objects educate and enlighten by demonstrating the adaptability of Jewish culture in different historical settings and geographical contexts.

The museum is open on Sunday-Thursday, 10:00am to 4:30pm, Friday, 10:00am to 4:00pm and Saturday, 1:00 to 4:30pm. There is no admission charge. For further information call (212) 744-1400 ext. 259.

Walk to Park Avenue, turn left and proceed to 67th Street. Turn right for...

Stop 146.

PARK EAST SYNAGOGUE
163 East 67th Street   Tel. (212) 737-6900

Organized in 1888, its 1890 Moorish Revival building was designed by architects Schneider and Herter. This synagogue was founded by Jews from southern Germany as an Orthodox congregation. It is one of the few synagogues in the city still owned by the same congregation which built it.

The Russion Mission to the United Nations was located directly across the street–in that white brick high rise apartment building. During the Cold War, many anti-Russian rallies were conducted in front of this synagogue. On several occasions, bombs were detonated by radical Jewish groups. The explosionss caused international incidents and also shattered the beautiful stained-glass windows of the synagogue.

Doubleback to Park Avenue, turn right and go to 78th Street. Turn left and proceed to No. 60 East 78th Street.

Stop 147.

RAMAZ UPPER SCHOOL
60 East 78th Street   Tel. (212) 427-1000

The Rabbi Joseph H. Lookstein School of Ramaz, a private Jewish Day School, is modern and progressive in its approach. religious and secular studies are alternated and, when possible, are correlated and integrated.

The architects of the Upper School, Conklin and Rossant, have designed a baffling façade. The angled windows on the upper level appear as a painter's garret and are actually used as the school's art studio. The arched forms (windows and pinnacles) appear as bay windows or can be interpreted to read as the domes of Jerusalem or the Tablets of the Law (Ten Commandments).

Park East Synagogue.

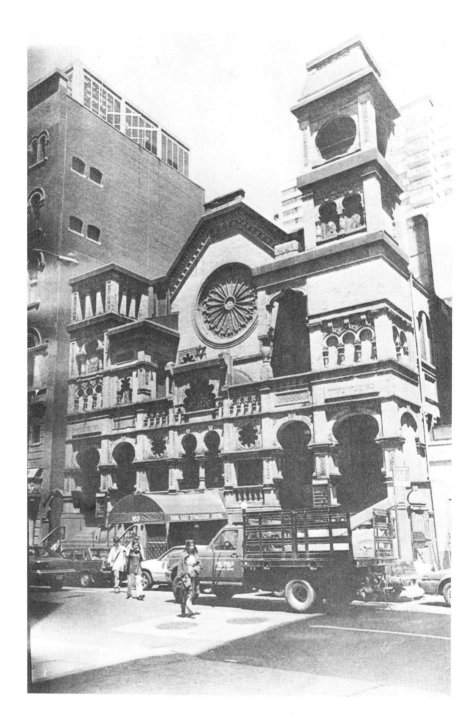

The Park East Synagogue on East 67th Street.

The Ramaz Lower School is located adjoining Congregation Kehilath Jeshurun (KJ), at 125 East 85th Street.

Go to Fifth Avenue, turn right and walk to 86th Street.

Stop 148.

YIVO INSTITUTE FOR JEWISH RESEARCH (former)
1048 Fifth Avenue

This building was built in 1914 for William Starr Miller. It was later the home of Mrs. Cornelius Vanderbilt. It was then sold to YIVO Institute. YIVO Institute for Jewish Research was founded in Vilna in 1925. It is recognized as the world center for Yiddish research. It has the most complete record of Jewish life in Eastern Europe. It was moved to New York in 1940 to escape the ravages of the Nazis. YIVO moved out of this beautiful building in 1995 and is scheduled to move into the new Center for Jewish History in early 1999. see **Stop. 122.**

Walk along 86th Street to Madison Avenue, turn left for...

Stop 149.

PARK AVENUE SYNAGOGUE
50 East 87th Street   Tel. (212) 369-2600

The Park Avenue Synagogue was founded in 1882 by a group of German and Hungarian Jews. It is today one of the city's prominent Conservative congregations. Its honorary rabbi, Judah Nadich was General Eisenhower's adviser on Jewish affairs in Germany.

The magnificent sculpture above the main entrance to the educational center on Madisin Avenue was designed by Nathan Rapaport. The eminent artist, Adolph Gottlieb, designed the stained-glass windows in the same building. The main sanctuary is designed in exquisite Moorish Revival.

Walk to Lexington Avenue, turn left and go to 91st Street.

Stop 150.

92nd STREET YMHA PERFORMING ARTS CENTER
1395 Lexington Avenue   Tel. (212) 996-1100

This is the largest and oldest Jewish Community Center in continuous existence in the United States. It was founded in 1874 and was built by the German-Jewish community, notably Jacob H. Schiff. The present main building was built in the 1920s and contains a gym, pool, craft classes, library, concert hall and dance studios.

This is the only YMHA in the country which contains dormitory facilities. The Y presents cultural programs such as chamber ensembles, ballet performances, and piano and violin recitals. There are lecture series which cater to singles and feature such personalities as Elie Wiesel and Dick Cavett.

Walk along 92nd Street toward Fifth Avenue.

Stop 151.

THE JEWISH MUSEUM
Fifth Avenue & 92nd Street   Tel. (212) 423-3200

The Jewish Museum began in 1904, when Judge Mayer Sulzberger included 26 objects as part of a gift of books and manuscripts to the Jewish Theological Seminary of America. These works of ceremonial and fine art were donated to "serve as a suggestion for the establishment of a Jewish Museum."

Until 1944, the growing collection was housed in the Seminary's library. In that year, Frieda Schiff Warburg, widow of the prominent philanthropist Fekix Warburg, donated the family mansion of Fifth Avenue at 92nd Street to the Seminary for use as the Jewish Museum. The 1908 residence, designed by C.P.H. Gilbert in the style of a French Gothic chateau, provided an elegant home for the collection.

At the heart of the Jewish Museum is its magnificent permanent collection, including more than 14,000 works of art and artifacts covering 4,000 years of Jewish history. The fine arts collection includes works by Rembrandt, Marc Chagall and George Segal. The collection of Jewish ceremonial art is the most comprehensive in the United States and one of the largest in the world with particularly fine collections of Chanukah lamps and ritual textiles.

Some of the past exhibitions presented by the Jewish Museum include: The Precious Legacy–Judaica Treasures from the Czechoslavakia State Collection, the Jews of Ethiopia, the Dreyfus Affair, the Jewish Heritage in American Folk Art and the Circle of Montparnasse–Jewish Artists of Paris 1905-1945.

A few years ago, the Jewish Museum restored its original building and constructed a new wing, designed by Kevin Roche. It doubled its gallery space, created new classrooms and workshops for educational programs, and provided essential improvements in public amenities such as a kosher cafe, a larger lobby and an expanded gift shop.

Walk north along Fifth Avenue to 98th Street.

The Jewish Museum is housed in a former chateau.
Courtesy of the Jewish Museum

Stop 152.

MOUNT SINAI HOSPITAL
Fifth Avenue, between 98th and 101st Streets

Jews' Hospital was incorporated in 1852 because of the need to prevent Jews from being approached by conversionists in the city hospitals. Opened in 1855 on 28th Street between 7th and 8th Avenues, the hospital admitted only Jews in its early years, except for accident cases. The hospital became non-sectarian in 1864 and the name was changed to Mount Sinai two years later.

Mount Sinai Hospital was built by the German-Jewish community. Because kosher food was not available at Mount Sinai Hospital, the Orthodox Jewish community which arrived in the Lower East Side in the 1880s, organized Beth Israel Hospital in 1890. It was the first hospital under Orthodox auspices.

In recent years, it is now possible to order kosher meals for patients in virtually every hospital in the city.

Places

of

Interest

Places of Interest

ABIGAIL ADAMS SMITH MUSEUM (1799)
421 East 61st Street   Tel. (212) 838-6878
Admission: $3 adults, $2 seniors/students
Hours: Tues-Sun 11:00-4:00 and Tues 11:00-9:00
Subway: N or R to Lexington Avenue; #4, #5, #6 to 59th Street

Built in 1799 as a coach house, the museum displays furniture and artifacts of the Federal period. There is a framed letter from George
Washington. A garden in the manner of the 18th century is planted
around the house. Abigail Adams Smith was the daughter of John
Quincy Adams.

ALICE AUSTEN HOUSE (Staten Island)
2 Hylan Boulevard   Tel. (718) 816-4506
Admission: $3 adults, $2 seniors/students
Hours: Thur-Sun 12:00-5:00
Staten Island Ferry Terminal then bus #S51 to Hylan Boulevard

Victorian cottage of documentary photographer Alice Austen.

ALTERNATIVE MUSEUM
594 Broadway (Houston Street)   Tel. (212) 966-4444
Admission: $3 (donation)
Hours: Tues-Sat 11:00-6:00
Subway: B, D, F, Q to Broadway-Lafayette; N, R to Prince Street

AMERICAN CRAFT MUSEUM
40 West 53rd Street   Tel. (212) 956-3535
Admission: $5 adults, $2.50 seniors/students
Hours: Tues-Sun 10:00-5:00, Tues 10:00-8:00
Subway: E, F to Fifth Avenue; #6 to 51st Street

Exhibits on glass, fiber, wood, clay, metal and paper by America's most
talented craftspeople.

AMAERICAN MUSEUM OF THE MOVING IMAGE (Queens)
35th Avenue & 36th Street   Tel. (718) 784-0077
Admission: $7 adults, $4 seniors/students
Hours: Tues-Fri 12:00-5:00, Sat-Sun 11:00-6:00
Subway: G or R to Steinway Street, N to 36th Avenue

There are more than 60,000 artifacts chronicling the art, history and
technology of motion pictures, television and videotapes. The museum

is housed in a renovated building on the site of the former Astoria Studios, a 1920s facility used by Paramount Pictures

AMERICAN MUSEUM OF NATURAL HISTORY
Central Park West & 79th Street   Tel. (212) 769-5100
Admission: $8 adults, $4 seniors/students (donation)
Extra charge for IMAX theater.
Hours: Sun-Thur 10:00-5:45, Fri-Sat 10:00-8:45
Subway: B, C to 81st Street

The American Museum of Natural History contains more than 34 million specimens and artifacts of gems, minerals, dinosaurs, reptiles, amphibians and sea-shells. Be sure to see the 90-foot fiberglass blue whale in the Hall of Ocean Life, the *Star of India* sapphire and a cross-section of a 1300-year-old sequoia. There are '"hands-on" exhibits in the Discovery Room and continuous films on natural, scientific and anthropological subjects in the Naturmax Theater.
Note: The adjoining Hayden Planetarium is presently closed while being rebuilt as a "state-of-the-art" structure and its new Center for Earth & Space.

AMERICAN NUMISMATIC SOCIETY
Broadway & 155th Street   Tel. (212) 234-3130
Admission: Free
Hours: Sun 1:00-4:00, Tues-Sat 9:00-4:30
Subway: #1/9 to 157th Street

The American Numismatic Society has more than 600,000 coins and medals from around the world in its collection. The second floor contains a library and exhibit rooms.

AMERICAS SOCIETY ART GALLERY
680 Park Avenue   Tel. (212) 249-8950
Admission: Free
Hours: Tues-Sun 12:00-6:00
Subway: #6 to 68th Street

ANTHOLOGY FILM ARCHIVES
32 Second Avenue   Tel. (212) 505-5181
Admission: $7 adults, $5 seniors/students
Subway: F to Second Avenue; #6 to Bleecker Street

AQUARIUM FOR WILDLIFE CONSERVATION (Brooklyn)
Surf Avenue at West 8th Street   Tel. (718) 265-FISH
Admission: $6.75 adults, $3 seniors/children
Hours: 10:00-5:00 daily
Subway: D or F to West 8th Street

The New York Aquarium is located in Coney Island. There are exhibits of marine life in outdoor and indoor tanks.

ASIA SOCIETY GALLERIES
725 Park Avenue   Tel. (212) 517-ASIA
Admission: $3 adults, $1 seniors/students
             Free on Thursday 6:00-8:00pm
Hours: Tues-Sat 11:00-6:00, Thur 11:00-8:00, Sun 12:00-5:00
Subway: #6 to 68th Street

The Asia Society presents Asian cultural programs and changing exhibits of Asian art.

THE BARD GRADUATE CENTER
FOR STUDIES IN THE DECORATIVE ARTS
18 West 86th Street   Tel. (212) 501-3000
Admission: $2 adults, $1 seniors/children
Subway: B or C to 86th Street

BARTOW-PELL MANSION, CARRIAGE HOUSE & GARDENS
895 Shore Road, Pelham Bay Park **(The Bronx)** Tel. (718) 885-1461
Admission: $2.50 adults, $1.25 seniors/children
Hours: Wed, Sat & Sun 12:00-4:00
Subway: #6 to Pelham Bay Park (then bus)

The site was bought from the Siwanoy Indians in 1654. The first house was destroyed during the Revolutionary War. The existing mansion was built in 1836. Furnished in period artifacts, it is the only home of its era in this region. There are beautiful gardens and views of the Long Island Sound.

BLACK FASHION MUSEUM
155 West 126th Street   Tel. (212) 666-1320
Admission: $3
Hours: Mon-Fri 12:00-6:00 (by appointment only)
Subway: #2, #3 to 125th Street

THE BRONX MUSEUM OF THE ARTS (The Bronx)
1040 Grand Concourse   Tel. (718) 681-6000
Admission: $3 adults, $2 seniors/children
Hours: Wed 3:00-9:00, Thur-Fri 10:00-5:00, Sat-Sun 1:00-6:00
Subway: D or #4 to161st Street

This building was originally designed for the Young Israel of the Concourse in the 1950s. In 1982, it was completely redesigned for the Bronx Museum of the Arts.

THE BRONX ZOO (The Bronx)
Tel. (718) 367-1010
Admission: $3 adults, $1.50 seniors/children
Hours: Daily 10:00-4:00
Subway: #2 to Pelham Parkway

The Bronx Zoo, also known as the New York Zoological Park, displays animals representing more than 600 species in naturalistic indoor environments and large outdoor habitats. Be sure to visit the *World of Birds*. Additional attractions include monorail and shuttle, children's zoo and camel rides.

BROOKLYN BOTANIC GARDEN (Brooklyn)
1000 Washington Avenue   Tel. (718) 622-4433
Admission: $3 adults, $1.50 seniors/children
Hours: Tues-Fri 8:00-6:00, Sat-Sun 10:00-6:00
Subway: D or Q to Prospect Park, #2 or #3 to Eastern Parkway

The 52 acres of the Brooklyn Botanic Garden were by the Olmsted Brothers (of Central Park and Prospect Park fame) in 1910 and include the Garden of Fragrance for the blind; Japanese Garden; the Conservatory, housing tropical plants and a bonsai museum under three glass pavilions.

BROOKLYN CHILDREN'S MUSEUM (Brooklyn)
145 Brooklyn Avenue   Tel. (718) 735-4403
Admission: $3
Hours: Wed-Fri 2:00-5:00, Sat-Sun 12:00-5:00
Subway: #3 to Kingston Avenue

Children can learn about how animals get their energy from food, visit a greenhouse or work with butterflies and fossils. They can use 20,000 cultural artifacts and natural history specimens from the museum's collection.

THE BROOKLYN HISTORICAL SOCIETY (Brooklyn)
128 Pierrepont Street   Tel. (718) 624-0890
Admission: $2.50 adults, $1 seniors/children
Hours: Tues-Sat 12:00-5:00
Subway: M, N, R to Court Street, A, C, F to Jay Street,
        #2, #3, #4, or #5 to Borough Hall

Built as the Long Island Historical Society in 1878 by George B. Post, when Brooklyn was an independent city on Long Island. The ground floor contains an exhibition hall. Be sure to visit the richly appointed library on the second (when restoration is completed).

BROOKLYN MUSEUM OF ART (Brooklyn)
200 Eastern Parkway   Tel. (718) 638-5000
Admission: $4 adults, $2 students, $1.50 seniors
Hours: Wed-Sun 10:00-5:00
Subway: #2 or #3 to Eastern Parkway

The Brooklyn Museum was designed in 1893 by McKim, Mead & White.
It houses collections of Egyptian art, primitive art, American paintings,
Colonial period rooms and an outdoor sculpture garden. The Brooklyn
Museum may be off the beaten track but is known as a world-class
museum.

CARNEGIE HALL (See **STOP. 129**)
881 Seventh Avenue (56th Street)   Tel. (212) 903-9790
Hours: Mon-Tues & Thur-Fri Tours at 11:30, 2:00, 3:00
Subway: N or R to 57th Street

CASTLE CLINTON NATIONAL MONUMENT (See **STOP. 1**)
Battery Park   Tel. (212) 344-7220
Admission: Free
Hours: Daily 9:00-6:00
Subway: #1/9 to South Ferry, #4, #5 to Bowling Green

CENTER FOR BOOK ARTS
626 Broadway (5th Floor)   Tel. (212) 460-9768
Admission: Free
Hours: Mon-Fri 10:00-6:00, Sat 10:00-4:00
Subway: N, R to Prince Street; #6 to Bleecker Street

CENTRAL PARK WILDLIFE CENTER & WILDLIFE GALLERY
Fifth Avenue & 64th Street   Tel. (212) 861-6030
Admission: $2.50 adults, $1.25 seniors, $ .50 children
            Gallery is free
Hours: Daily 10:00-4:30
Subway: N or R to Fifth Avenue, #6 to 68th Street

The Central Park Zoo was recently redesigned to eliminate the "caged-
in" effect. Instead, the people are led through various walkways and view
the animals in naturalistic surroundings.

CHAIM GROSS STUDIO MUSEUM
526 LaGuardia Place   Tel. (212) 529-4906
Admission: Free
Hours: Sat 12:00-6:00 or by appointment
Subway: A, B, D, E, F, Q to West 4th Street or #6 to Bleecker Street

CHILDREN'S MUSEUM OF THE ARTS
72 Spring Street   Tel. (212) 941-9198
Admission: $5 weekends, $4 weekdays, Seniors free.
Hours: Thur-Fri 1:00-7:00, Sat-Sun 11:00-5:00
Subway: N or R to Prince Street, #6 to Spring Street

CHILDREN'S MUSEUM OF MANHATTAN
212 West 83rd Street   Tel. (212) 721-1223
Admission: $5 adults, $2.50 seniors/children
Hours: Mon, Wed, Thur 1:30-5:30, Fri, Sat, Sun 10:00-5:00
Subway: #1/9 to 86th Street

The Children's Museum of Manhattan is an educational playground of interactive exhibitions and activity centers. Kids can make their own video productions, newscasts and public affairs programs.

CHINA INSTITUTE OF AMERICA
125 East 65th Street   Tel. (212) 744-8181
Admission: $5 contribution
Hours: Mon-Sat 10:00-5:00, Tues 10:00-8:00
Subway: N or R to Lexington Avenue, #6 to 68th Street

There are changing exhibits on Chinese fine arts and folk traditions.

CITY HALL   (See STOP. 42)
Broadway & Murray Street   Tel. (212) 669-4506
Admission: Free
Hours: Mon-Fri 9:00-5:00
Subway: N or R to City Hall, #4, #5, #6 to Brooklyn Bridge

THE CLOISTERS
Fort Tryon Park   Tel. (212) 923-3700
Admission: $7 adults, $3.50 children
Hours: Tues-Sun 9:30-4:45
Subway: A to 190th Street

The Cloisters is a branch of the Metropolitan Museum of Art. It was named for the French and Spanish monastic cloisters imported and reassembled in Fort Tryon Park in concert with a 12th century chapter house, Fuentaduena Chapel, and a Gothic and a Romanesque chapel. The highest point in Manhattan, 165 feet above sea level, is at Fort Washington Avenue and 190th Street. There are great views of the Hudson River and the Palisades (in New Jersey) from this Washington Heights location.

COMMODITIES EXCHANGE CENTER - Visitor's Gallery
4 World Trade Center   Tel. (212) 938-2025

CONFERENCE HOUSE (Staten Island)
Hylan Boulevard   Tel. (718) 984-2086
Admission: Donation
Hours: Wed-Sun
Staten Island Ferry then SIRT to last stop in Tottenville

This was the site of the only Revolutionary War peace conference. The stone manor was built in 1675.

COOPER-HEWITT MUSEUM - NATIONAL DESIGN MUSEUM
2 East 91st Street   Tel. (212) 860-6860
Admission: $3 adults, $1.50 seniors/children (Tues evening-Free)
Hours: Tues 10:00-9:00, Wed-Sat 10:00-5:00, Sun 12:00-5:00
Subway: #6 to 86th or 96th Street

The Cooper-Hewett Museum is a branch of the Smithsonian Institute of Washington, D.C. It is housed in the former Andrew Carnegie house which was designed in 1901 by Babb, Cook & Willard. The permanent collection encompasses textiles dating back 3000 years, jewelry, furniture, wallpaper, metalware, glassware and earthenware. The collection also includes the single largest group of architectural drawings in America.

DAHESH MUSEUM
601 Fifth Avenue   Tel. (212) 759-0606
Admission: Free
Hours: Tues-Sat 11:00-6:00
Subway: #6 to 51st Street

The Dahesh Museum features 19th and 20th century European art.

DIA CENTER FOR THE ARTS
548 West 22nd Street   Tel. (212) 989-5912
Admission: $3 donation
Hours: Thur-Sun 12:00-6:00
Subway: C or E to 23rd Street

DIA CENTER FOR THE ARTS
141 Wooster Street   Tel. (212) 473-8072
Admission: Free
Hours: Wed-Sat 12:00-6:00
Subway: C or E to Spring Street

DIA CENTER FOR THE ARTS
393 West Broadway   Tel. (212) 925-9397
Admission: Free

Hours: Wed-Sat 12:00-6:00
Subway: N or R to Prince Street

THE DRAWING CENTER
35 Wooster Street Tel. (212) 219-2166
Hours: Tues-Fri 10:00-6:00, Sat 11:00-6:00
Subway: N or R to Canal Street

DYCKMAN HOUSE (1783)
Broadway & 204th Street Tel. (212) 304-9422
Hours: Tues-Sat 11:00-4:00
Subway: A to 207th Street

The Dyckman House is the last 18th century Dutch Colonial farmhouse in Manhattan. The house shows strong Dutch influence with its gambral roof and brick and fieldstone lower walls. The interior contains random-width chestnut floors and original family furnishings.

ELDRIDGE STREET NATIONAL HISTORIC SYNAGOGUE
14 Eldridge Street Tel. (212) 219-0888 (See **STOP. 51**)
Admission: $4 adults, $2.50 seniors/students
Hours: Sun 11:00-4:00, Tues-Thur - tours given at 11:30 & 2:30
Subway: F to East Broadway, B or D to Grand Street

ELLIS ISLAND - MUSEUM OF IMMIGRATION (See **STOP. 5**)
Tel. (212) 269-5755
Admission: (Ferry) $7 adults, $3 children under 17
Hours: Daily 9:30-3:30
Ferry located in Castle Clinton - Battery Park
Subway: #1/9 to South Ferry, N or R to Whitehall Street

EMPIRE STATE BUILDING (Observation Deck)
350 Fifth Avenue Tel. (212) 736-3100
Admission: $6 adults, $3 seniors/students
Hours: Daily 9:30-midnight
Subway: B, D, F, Q, N, R to 34th Street, #6 to 33rd Street

Built during the Depression, the Empire State Building was once the tallest building in the world. It measures 1250 feet up to its dirigible mooring mast, which has since been replaced with a massive television antenna. The final scenes in the original *King Kong* movie of 1931 showed that round-topped dirigible mast which the gorilla held onto. The Empire State Building was designed by Shreve, Lamb & Harmon in 1931. Be sure to see the exquisite Art Deco designs behind the information desk at the Fifth Avenue entrance.

THE EQUITABLE GALLERY
787 Seventh Avenue   Tel. (212) 554-4818
Admission: Free
Hours: Mon-Fri 11:00-6:00, Sat 12:00-5:00
Subway: #1/9 to 50th Street

FEDERAL HALL NATIONAL MONUMENT   (See STOP. 31)
26 Wall Street   Tel. (212) 264-8711
Admission: Free
Hours: Mon-Fri 9:00-5:00
Subway: #2, #3, #4, #5, to Wall Street, J, M, Z to Broad Street

FEDERAL RESERVE BANK (See STOP. 35)
33 Liberty Street   Tel. (212) 720-6130
Admission: Free
Hours: Tours are given at 10:30, 11:30, 1:30, 2:30
Subway: #2, #3, #4, #5, J, M, Z to Fulton Street

FORBES MAGAZINE GALLERIES
62 Fifth Avenue   Tel. (212) 206-5549
Admission: Free
Hours: Tues-Wed, Fri-Sat 10:00-4:00
Subway: N or R to Union Square, #4, #5, #6 to 14th Street

This is the place to see twelve Faberge´ Easter eggs, the world's largest private collection of these priceless objects created for the Czars of Russia. There are also over five hundred toy boats, 12,000 toy soldiers, a collection of Presidential Papers, historical documents and model rooms.

FRAUNCES TAVERN MUSEUM
54 Pearl Street   Tel. (212) 425-1778   (See STOP. 25)
Admission: $2.50 adults, $1.50 seniors/students
Hours: Mon-Fri 10:00-4:45, Sat 12:00-4:00
Subway: N or R to Whitehall Street, #1/9 to South Ferry

FRICK COLLECTION
One East 70th Street   Tel. (212) 288-0700
Admission: $5 adults, $3 seniors/students
Hours: Tues-Sat 10:00-6:00, Sun 1:00-6:00
Subway: N or R to Fifth Avenue, #6 to 68th Street

The Frick Collection is housed in the former mansion of Henry Clay Frick, chairman of the Carnegie Steel Corporation. It was built in 1914 and became a museum in 1935 with renovations by John Russell Pope. There are paintings by Monet, Hals, Whistler, Limoges enamels, Oriental rugs, porcelains and sculptures. It has been said that the Frick Collection is the most relaxing place in the city, especially the glass-covered courtyard and fountain.

GRACIE MANSION (Tours)
East End Avenue & 88th Street   Tel. (212) 570-4751
Admission: $4 adults, $3 seniors
Hours: Tours given on Wednesdays by reservation only.
Subway: #4, #5, #6 to 86th Street

Gracie Mansion is the official residence of the Mayor of New York City. It was built in 1799 as the Archibald Gracie House.

GRANT'S TOMB NATIONAL MEMORIAL
Riverside Drive & 122nd Street   Tel. (212) 666-1640
Admission: Free
Hours: Wed-Sun 9:00-5:00
Subway: #1/9 to 116th Street

A massive granite mausoleum set on a hill overlooking the Hudson River. General Ulysses S. Grant and his wife *are* buried here. There is an exhibit pertaining to Grant's life as a General and as the President of the United States.

GREEK JEWISH MUSEUM (See STOP. 89)
280 Broome Street   Tel. (212)431-1619
Admission: Donation
Hours: Sun 11:00-4:00
Subway: F to Delancey Street, J, M, Z to Essex Street

GREY ART GALLERY & STUDENT CENTER
33 Washington Place   Tel. (212) 998-6780
Admission: Free
Hours: Tues, Thur, Fri 11:00-6:30, Wed 11:00-8:30, Sat 11;00-5:00
Subway: #6 to Astor Place, N or R to 8th Street

SOLOMON R. GUGGENHEIM MUSEUM
1071 Fifth Avenue (88th Street)   Tel. (212) 423-3500
Admission: $15 adults, $10 seniors/students
Hours: Sun-Wed 10:00-6:00, Fri-Sat 10:00-8:00
Subway: #4, #5, #6 to 86th Street

The Solomon R. Guggenheim Museum was designed by Frank Lloyd Wright in 1959. Take the elevator to the top floor and work your way down. Paintings are hung along the spiraled walkway.

GUGGENHEIM MUSEUM SOHO
575 Broadway (Prince Street) Tel. (212) 423-3500
Admission: $8 adults, $5 seniors/students
Hours: Sun & Wed-Fri 11:00-6:00, Sat 11:00-8:00
Subway: N or R to Prince Street, #6 to Spring Street

GUINNESS WORLD RECORDS EXHIBIT HALL
350 Fifth Avenue   Tel. (212) 947-2335
Admission: $7 adults, $6 seniors
Hours: Daily 9:00-10:00
Subway: B, D, F, Q, N, R to 34th Street

The Guinness World Records Exhibit Hall is located on the Concourse
level of the Empire State Building. There are exhibits, dioramas, videotapes, replicas and photographs documenting all of these events.

HALL OF FAME NATIONAL MEMORIAL (The Bronx)
University Avenue & Hall of Fame Terrace   Tel. (718) 220-6003
Admission: Free
Hours: Daily 9:00-5:00
Subway: #4 to Burnside Avenue

The Hall of Fame is located on the campus of Bronx Community
College.

HAMILTON GRANGE NATIONAL MEMORIAL (1802)
287 Convent Avenue   Tel. (212) 283-5154
Hours: Closed Mon & Tues
Subway: #1/9 to 145th Street

The area of Hamilton Heights was once the country estate of Alexander
Hamilton, whose house, the Grange, stands at Convent Avenue and
141st Street, next to St. Luke's. Alexander Hamilton was the first United
States Secretary of the Treasury.

THE HARBOR DEFENSE MUSEUM (Brooklyn)
230 Fort Hamilton   Tel. (718) 630-4349
Admission: Free
Hours: Tues-Thur 10:00-2:00
Subway: R to 95th Street

Fort Hamilton was originally built before the War of 1812 on the small
island which today supports the eastern tower of the Verrazano-Narrows
Bridge. The present Fort Hamilton was built from 1825 to 1831. There
are still some original cannons and artillery along Fourth Avenue at
Shore Road.

HAYDEN PLANETARIUM (Under Construction)
Columbus Avenue & 81st Street   Tel. (212) 769-5100

HISPANIC SOCIETY OF AMERICA
Broadway & 155th Street   Tel. (212) 690-0743
Admission: Free
Hours: Tues-Sat 10:00-4:30, Sun 1:00-4:00
Subway: A or B to 155th Street

See paintings of the Old Masters: El Greco, Goya, Velazquez, archaeological finds, ceramics and other decorative arts from the Iberian penin-
sula.

INTERNATIONAL CENTER OF PHOTOGRAPHY (ICP)
Fifth Avenue & 94th Street   Tel. (212) 860-1777
1133 Avenue of the Americas Tel. (212) 768-4682
Admission: $4 adults, $2.50 seniors/children
Hours: Wed-Sun 11:00-6:00, Tues 11:00-8:00
Subway: #6 to 96th Street

This museum is devoted exclusively to photography. There are changing
exhibits, workshops and photo labs.

INTERNATIONAL CENTER OF PHOTOGRAPHY (ICP)
1133 Avenue of the Americas (43rd Street) Tel. (212) 768-4682
Admission: $4 adults, $2.50 seniors/children
Hours: Wed-Sun 11:00-6:00, Tues 11:00-8:00
Subway: B, D, F, Q to 42nd Street, N or R to Times Square

U.S.S. INTREPID SEA-AIR-SPACE MUSEUM
12th Avenue & 46th Street   Tel. (212) 245-2533
Admission: $10 adults, $7.50 seniors/veterans
Hours: Wed-Sun 10:00-5:00
Subway: Any subway to 42nd Street (Times Square) then walk west.
The U.S.S. Intrepid, an aircraft carrier used in World War II and Vietnam,
was a space program recovery ship as well as an antisubmarine carrier
before being converted into a museum. The 900-foot flight deck has historic aircraft which can be inspected. Visitors can climb through the con-
trol bridges and command centers of the carrier. Below deck are
antiques and film clips of flying machines from the turn of the century
through the 1930s.

THE ISAMU NOGUCHI GARDEN MUSEUM (Queens)
32-37 Vernon Boulevard (Long Island City) Tel. (718) 721-1932
Admission: $4 adults, $2 seniors/students
Hours: Wed-Fri 10:00-5:00, Sat-Sun 11:00-6:00
Subway: N to Broadway

This museum is dedicated to the work of a single artist, Isamu Noguchi (1904-88). There are sculptural displays in 12 galleries and an outdoor garden.

JAPAN SOCIETY
333 East 47th Street   Tel. (212) 832-1155
Admission: $3 donation
Hours: Tues-Sun 11:00-5:00
Subway: #6 to 51st Street, E or F to Lexington Avenue

THE JEWISH MUSEUM
Fifth Avenue & 92nd Street   Tel. (212) 423-3200 **(See STOP. 151)**
Admission: $7 adults, $5 seniors/students
Hours: Sun-Thur 11:00-5:45 (Free Tues evenings)
Subway: #6 to 86th Street

JEWISH THEOLOGICAL SEMINARY   (See STOP. 138)
3080 Broadway (122nd Street)   Tel. (212) 678-8082
Admission: Free
Hours: Sun-Thur 9:30-5:30, Fri 9:30-2:30
Subway: #1/9 to 116th Street

Changing exhibits on the first and fifth floors of the library wing.

JUDAICA MUSEUM (The Bronx)
5961 Palisade Avenue   Tel. (718) 548-548-1006

The Judaica Museum is located the Riverdale section in the Hebrew Home for the Aged.

KINGSLAND HOMESTEAD   See **Queens Historical Society**

LEO BAECK INSTITUTE
129 East 73rd Street   Tel. (212) 744-6400
Admission: Free
Hours: Mon-Thur 9:30-4:30, Fri 9:30-2:30
Subway: #6 to 68th Street

LIBRARY & MUSEUM OF THE PERFORMING ARTS
111 Amsterdam Avenue   Tel. (212) 870-1630
Admission: Free
Hours: Mon, Wed-Sat 12:00-6:00, Mon & Thur 6:00-8:00
        Tours are given Wed at 3:00
Subway: #1/9 to 66th Street

The two galleries at this branch of the New York Public Library show costume and set designs, music scores and other tools of the trade. The library is equipped with state-of-the-art audio equipment and a vast collection of recordings.

LINCOLN CENTER
FOR THE PERFORMING ARTS (Tours)
140 West 65th Street   Tel. (212) 877-1800

LOWER EAST SIDE TENEMENT MUSEUM
Orchard & Broome Streets   Tel. (212) 431-0233 **(See STOP. 88)**
Admission: $8 adults, $6 seniors/students
Hours: Tues-Sun 11:00-5:00
Subway: F to Delancey Street, J, M, Z to Essex Street

LUBAVITCHER REBBE MUSEUM (Brooklyn)
770 Eastern Parkway   Tel. (718) 953- 5244
By appointment only.

Visit the Lubavitch Hassidic community in Crown Heights. Part of the tour includes a visit to the World Headquarters building and bais hamedrash, a mikveh, a matzoh factory (depending upon time of year of your visit) and a museum and private library devoted specifically to the lives of the past Lubavitcher Rebbes.

MERCHANTS HOUSE MUSEUM
29 East 4th Street   Tel. (212) 777-1089
Admission: $3
Hours: Sun-Thur 1:00-4:00
Subway: D or F to Broadway-Lafayette

Tour of 19th century historic home.

METROPOLITAN MUSEUM OF ART (The Met)
Fifth Avenue & 82nd Street   Tel. (212) 879-5500
Admission: $7 adults, $3.50 seniors/students
Hours: Tues-Thur & Sun 9:30-5:15, Fri-Sat 9:30-8:45
Subway: #4, #5, #6 to 86th Street

The Metropolitan Museum of Art is a world-class museum. If you want to see every exhibit in the museum it would take several days! Among the collections are Egyptian, Greek and Roman art; Near Eastern art and antiquities; European and Oriental paintings and sculpture; arms and armor; musical instruments; ancient glass; and European and American decorative arts. Be sure to visit the most comprehensive art bookstore in the city, located on the main level.

METROPOLITAN OPERA (Backstage Tours)
Columbus Avenue & 65th Street Tel. (212) 582-3512

MORRIS-JUMEL MANSION (1765)
1765 Jumel Terrace Tel. (212) 923-8008
Admission: $3 adults, $2 seniors/students
Hours: Wed-Sun 10:00-4:00
Subway: B to 163rd Street

George Washington used this building as his headquarters in 1776.

THE MUNICIPAL ART SOCIETY
457 Madison Avenue Tel. (212) 935-3960
Admission: Free
Hours: Daily 11:00-5:00 (Closed Thur & Sun)
Subway: E or F to Fifth Avenue, #6 to 51st Street

The best architecture bookstore in town is located here.

EL MUSEO DEL BARIO
1230 Fifth Avenue Tel. (212) 831-7272
Admission: $4 adults, $2 seniors/students
Hours: Wed-Sun 11:00-5:00
Subway: #6 to 103rd Street

THE MUSEUM AT THE FASHION INSTITUTE OF TECHNOLOGY
Seventh Avenue at 27th Street Tel. (212) 760-7760
Admission: Free
Hours: Tues-Fri 12:00-8:00, Sat 10:00-5:00
Subway: C or E to 23rd Street

MUSEUM FOR AFRICAN ART
593 Broadway Tel. (212) 966-1313
Admission: $4 adults, $2 seniors/students
Hours: Tues-Fri 10:30-5:30, Sat-Sun 12:00-6:00
Subway: N or R to Prince Street, #6 to Spring Street

MUSEUM OF AMERICAN FINANCIAL HISTORY
24 Broadway (Bowling Green) Tel. (212) 908-4110
Admission: Free
Hours: Mon-Fri 11:30-2:30
Subway: N or R to Whitehall Street, #4 or #5 to Bowling Green

MUSEUM OF AMERICAN FOLK ART
2 Lincoln Square Tel. (212) 595-9533

Admission: Free
Hours: Tues-Sun 11:30-7:30
Subway: #1/9 to 66th Street

The best of American folk art, from the 18th century to the present; paintings, sculpture, textiles, furniture and decorative arts. The museum holds regular lectures and workshops.

MUSEUM OF AMERICAN ILLUSTRATION
128 East 63rd Street   Tel. (212) 838-2560
Admission: Free
Hours: Sat 12:00-4:00, Tues 10:00-8:00, Wed-Fri 10:00-5:00
Subway: N or R to Lexington Avenue, #4, #5, #6 to 59th Street

The Museum of American Illustration displays changing exhibits by noted illustrators of the past and present. Lectures and special demonstrations are also held.

MUSEUM OF THE AMERICAN PIANO
211 West 58th Street   Tel. (212) 246-4646
Admission: $15
Hours: By appointment only
Subway: N or R to 57th Street

This museum has an exhibit on the history of keyboards to 1846. The tour includes a lecture and mini-concert.

MUSEUM OF CHINESE IN THE AMERICAS
70 Mulberry Street   Tel. (212) 619-4785
Admission: $3 adults, $1 seniors/students
Hours: Tues-Sun 10:30-5:00
Subway: B, D, Q to Grand Street

MUSEUM OF THE CITY OF NEW YORK
Fifth Avenue & 103rd Street   Tel. (212) 534-1672
Admission: $5 adults, $4 seniors/students
Hours: Wed-Sat 10:00-5:00, Sun 1:00-5:00
Subway: #6 to 103rd Street

The Museum of the City of New York is devoted to the life and history of the city. The story of New York City is told through historical paintings, Currier & Ives prints, period rooms, costumes, Tiffany silver, ship models and toys and dolls. John D. Rockefeller's bedroom and dressing room were taken from his mansion at Fifth Avenue and 54th Street when it was demolished in 1937 and is now on display in the museum.

MUSEUM OF JEWISH HERITAGE
A LIVING MEMORIAL TO THE HOLOCAUST (See STOP. 16)
18 First Place (Battery Park City) Tel. (212) 786-0820
Admission: $7 adults, $5 seniors/students
Hours: Sun-Fri 9:00-5:00, Thur 9:00-8:00
          (in winter: Fri 9:00-1:00)
Subway: #4, #5 to Bowling Green, N or R to Whitehall Street
          #1/9 to South Ferry

MUSEUM OF MODERN ART (MOMA)
11 West 53rd Street   Tel. (212) 708-9480
Admission: $8.50 adults, $5.50 seniors/students
Hours: Sat-Tues 11:00-6:00, Thur-Fri 12:00-8:30
Subway: E or F to Fifth Avenue

The Museum of Modern Art offers a survey of 20th century paintings, sculptures, drawings, prints, photographs, architectural models and plans, design objects, films and videotapes, Classic, artistic and documentary movies are shown Thursday through Tuesday.

MUSEUM OF TELEVISION & RADIO
25 West 52nd Street   Tel. (212) 621-6600
Admission: $6 adults, $4 seniors/students
Hours: Tues-Sun 12:00-6:00, Thur 12:00-8:00, Fri 12:00-9:00
Subway: E or F to Fifth Avenue

The Museum of Television and Radio maintains a collection of 20,000 radio and television program tapes spanning the history of American and foreign broadcasting. Visitors can select material from a computerized file, then watch or listen to it in one of 23 booths. There are also changing exhibits, workshops and presentations.

NATIONAL ACADEMY OF DESIGN
Fifth Avenue & 89th Street   Tel. (212) 369-4880
Admission: $3.50 adults, $2 seniors/students
Hours: Wed-Sun 12:00-5:00, Fri 12:00-8:00
Subway: #4, #5, #6 to 86th Street

The National Academy of Design displays a permanent collection of artworks, as well as changing architectural exhibits, drawings, paintings and sculptures.

NATIONAL MUSEUM
OF THE AMERICAN INDIAN (Smithsonian) (See STOP. 12)
U.S. Customs House at One Bowling Green   Tel. (212) 825-6992
Admission: Free

Hours: Daily 10:00-5:00
Subway: #4, #5 to Bowling Green

The National Museum of the American Indian is concerned with the pre-historic Western Hemisphere and the contemporary American Indian. The museum is part of the Smithsonian Institute of Washington, D.C.

THE NATIONAL MUSEUM OF CATHOLIC ARTS & HISTORY
630 Fifth Avenue   Tel. (212) 752-3785
Subway: E or F to Fifth Avenue

NBC TOURS
30 Rockefeller Plaza   Tel. (212) 664-7174

NEW MUSEUM OF CONTEMPORARY ART
583 Broadway   Tel. (212) 219-1355
Admission: $4 adults, $3 seniors/students
Hours: Wed-Fri & Sun 12:00-6:00, Sat 12:00-8:00
Subway: N or R to Prince Street

The New Museum of Contemporary Arts displays works showing the development of emerging artists and focusing on experimental ideas.

THE NEWSEUM
580 Madison Avenue   Tel. (212) 317-7596
Admission: Free
Hours: Mon-Sat 10:00-5:30
Subway: N or R to Fifth Avenue

NEW YORK ACADEMY OF MEDICINE
1216 Fifth Avenue (103rd Street)   Tel. (212) 876-8200
Admission: Free
Hours: Mon-Fri 9:00-5:00
Subway: #6 to 103rd Street

The New York Academy of Medicine contains classic manuscripts and books from the history of medicine. It is located just north of Mount Sinai Hospital, the city's first Jewish hospital. (See **STOP. 152**)

THE NEW YORK BOTANICAL GARDEN (The Bronx)
200th Street at Southern Boulevard
Admission: $3 adults, $1 seniors/students
Hours: Tues-Sun 10:00-4:00
Subway: D to Bedford Park Boulevard

This is one of the world's largest botanical gardens, covering 250 acres.

The garden has 16 specialty gardens as well as 40 acres of original forest and the Enid A. Haupt Conservatory. A tram ride through the garden is available. Be sure to see the model railroads assembled during the Chanukah and New Year season.

NEW YORK CITY FIRE MUSEUM
278 Spring Street   Tel. (212) 691-1303
Admission: $4 adults, $2 seniors/students
Hours: Tues-Sun 10:00-4:00
Subway: #1/9 to Houston Street

The New York City Fire Museum displays the combined collection of fire memorabilia from the New York City Fire Department and the Home Insurance Company. The 1904 Beaux Arts style firehouse has firefighting vehicles and tools from Colonial days to the present, as well as displays on infamous fires, the firefighter and the history of fire insurance. Be sure to see the lone surviving fire watchtower located 121st Street near Madison in Harlem's Marcus Garvey (originally Mount Morris) Park. The city once had hundreds of similar fire watchtowers. This sole survivor was built in 1856.

NEW YORK CITY POLICE MUSEUM
235 East 20th Street   Tel. (212) 477-9753
Admission: Free
Hours: Mon-Fri 9:00-2:00
Subway: #6 to 23rd Street

The New York City Police Museum houses police memorabilia and emergency service displays. Be sure to see the old Police Headquarters located at 240 Centre Street. It was designed by Hoppin & Koen in 1909 in Renaissance Revival style. In 1988, it was renovated into 55 residential apartments. The new copper dome was installed by the French artisans who restored the Statue of Liberty's copper torch before its Centennial celebration in 1986.

NEW YORK HALL OF SCIENCE (Queens)
47-01 111th Street   Tel. (718) 699-0005
Admission: $4.50 adults, $3 seniors/students (Free Wed-Thur 2:00-5:00)
Hours: Wed-Sun 10:00-5:00
Subway: #7 to 111th Street

The New York Hall of Science is located in Flushing Meadow Park, site of the 1939 and 1964 World's Fairs. It was built as a science pavilion for the 1964 fair. It is a "hands-on" science and technology museum with a collection of 150 interactive exhibits focusing on color, light, microbiology, structures, feedback and quantum physics.

NEW-YORK HISTORICAL SOCIETY (See Stop. 135)
170 Central Park West   Tel. (212) 873-3400
Admission: $3 adults, $1 seniors/students
Hours: Wed-Sun 12:00-5:00
Subway: B or C to 81st Street

The New-York Historical Society galleries contain wall-to-wall silver objects, rare maps, antique toys, watercolors by John James Audobon and landscapes by members of the Hudson River School. The library upstairs is one of the major reference libraries of American history.

NEW YORK PUBLIC LIBRARY   (See STOP. 143)
Fifth Avenue & 42nd Street   Tel. (212) 869-8089
Admission: Free
Hours: Mon, Thur, Sat 10:00-6:00, Tues-Wed 11:00-6:00
Subway: B, D, F, Q to 42nd Street

NEW YORK STOCK EXCHANGE (Tours) (See STOP. 30)
20 Broad Street   Tel. (212) 656-5167
Admission: Free
Hours: Mon-Fri 9:15-4:00
Subway: #2, #3, #4, #5 to Wall Street, M, J, Z to Broad Street

NEW YORK TRANSIT MUSEUM (Brooklyn)
Boerum Place & Schermerhorn Street   Tel. (718) 243-5839
Admission: $3 adults, $1.50 seniors/students
Hours: Tues, Thur, Fri 10:00-4:00, Wed 10:00-6:00,
         Sat-Sun 12:00-5:00
Subway: #2, #3, #4, #5 to Borough Hall

The New York Transit Museum is located in a former subway station. There are photographs, artifacts and memorabilia that trace the development of the city's bus and subway systems on the mezzanine level of the former station. On the lower or track level are several vintage and restored subway cars dating back to the early part of this century.
There are plans to restore the city's first and grand subway station located beneath City Hall in Manhattan, and turn it into part of this New York Transit Museum. The museum has gift shops located in Grand Central Terminal and in Pennsylvania Station.

NEW YORK UNEARTHED (See STOP. 19)
(South Street Seaport Museum)
17 State Street   Tel. (212) 748-8628

Admission: Free
Hours: Mon-Sat 12:00-6:00
Subway: N or R to Whitehall Street, #1/9 to South Ferry

92nd STREET YMHA
CENTER FOR THE PERFORMING ARTS (See **STOP. 150**)
Lexington Avenue & 92nd Street Tel. (212) 996-1105

NORTH WIND UNDERSEA MUSEUM (The Bronx)
610 City Island Avenue Tel. (212) 885-0701
Admission: $3 adults, $2 seniors/students
Hours: Mon-Fri 12:00-4:00, Sat-Sun 12:00-5:00
Subway: #6 to Pelham Bay Park then bus BX12 to City Island

THE PAINE WEBER ART GALLERY
1285 Avenue of the Americas Tel. (212) 713-2885
Admission: Free
Hours: Mon-Fri 8:00-6:00
Subway: B, D, F, Q to Rockefeller Center

PIERPONT MORGAN LIBRARY
29 East 36th Street Tel. (212) 685-0610
Admission: $7 adults, $5 seniors/students
Hours: Tues-Fri 10:30-5:00, Sat 10:30-6:00, Sun 12:00-6:00
Subway: #6 to 33rd Street

The collection of J.P. Morgan is housed in this 1913 palazzo designed by McKim, Mead & White. The collection includes more than 1000 illuminated Medieval and Renaissance manuscripts, examples of fine bookbinding, from Gutenberg to modern times, and autographed manuscripts, both literary and musical.

EDGAR ALLAN POE COTTAGE (The Bronx)
Grand Concourse & Kingsbridge Road Tel. (718) 881-8900
Admission: $2
Hours: Sat 10:00-4:00, Sun 1:00-5:00
Subway: D to Kingsbridge Road

The 1816 house was moved into the park from its original site across Kingsbridge Road in 1913. It was occupied by Edgar Allan Poe 1846-49. It is furnished as it was in Poe's time and contains a few of his belongings. The museum displays many of Poe's manuscripts and other memorabilia.

PROSPECT PARK WILDLIFE CONSERVATION CENTER (Brooklyn)
450 Flatbush Avenue Tel. (718) 399-7339

Admission: $2.50 adults, $1.25 seniors/students
Hours: Daily 10:00-5:00
Subway: D, Q to Prospect Park

QUEENS BOTANICAL GARDEN (Queens)
43-50 Main Street Te, (718) 886-3800
Admission: Free
Hours: Mon-Fri 8:00-6:00, Sat-Sun 8:00-7:00
Subway: #7 to Main Street

QUEENS COUNTY FARM MUSEUM (Queens)
73-50 Little Neck Parkway Tel. (718) 347-3276
Admission: Free
Hours: Mon-Fri 9:00-5:00, Sat-Sun 10:00-5:00
Subway: E or F to Kew Gardens-Union Turnpike then bus Q46

QUEENS HISTORICAL SOCIETY (Queens)
143-35 37th Avenue Tel. (718) 939-0647
Admission: $2 adults, $1 seniors/students
Hours: Tues, Sat-Sun 2:30-4:30
Subway: #7 to Main Street

The Queens Historical Society is housed in a landmark building, the Kingsland Homestead, which was built in 1785.

QUEENS MUSEUM OF ART (Queens)
Flushing Meadow Park Tel. (718) 592-9700
Admission: $3 adults, $1.50 seniors/students
Hours: Wed-Fri 10:00-5:00, Sat-Sun 12:00-5:00
Subway: #7 to Willetts Point - Shea Stadium

The Queens Museum of Art is housed in the old New York City building constructed for New York's 1939 World's Fair. It was used as the meeting hall for the League of Nations, before the United Nations was established. For the 1964-65 World's Fair (located in the same Flushing Meadow Park) a magnificent panorama of New York City was designed, including every major street, building, bridge and park in the city. It was recently updated with many of the more recent skyscrapers and housing developments.

RADIO CITY MUSIC HALL (Backstage Tours)
Sixth Avenue & 50th Street Tel. (212) 632-4041

RICHMONDTOWN RESTORATION (Staten Island)
441 Clarke Avenue Tel. (718) 351-1611
Admission: $4 adults, $2.50 seniors/students
Hours: Wed-Sun 1:00-5:00
Staten Island Ferry then bus S74.

The Richmondtown Restoration is a collection of twenty buildings set on 100 acres designed as a village that recreates the appearance and lifestyle of three centuries of local history. Some of the buildings include the 17th century Voorlezer House (1695), the oldest surviving elementary school; the General Store (1840); and the Bennet House (1839), which houses the Museum of Childhood. There are demonstrations of Early American trades and crafts, and working kitchens with cooking in progress.

THEODORE ROOSEVELT BIRTHPLACE (1858)
28 East 20th Street   Tel. (212) 260-1616
Admission: $2 adults
Hours: Wed-Sun 9:00-5:00
Subway: N or R to Union Square, #4, #5, #6 to 14th Street

This is the reconstructed house of the only President born in New York City. It was his home 1858-75. Four floors contain mid-19th century furnishings and items pertaining to Roosevelt's professional and recreational pursuits.

THE SKYSCRAPER MUSEUM
44 Wall Street   Tel. (212) 968-1961
Admission: Free
Hours: Tues-Sat
Subway: #2, #3, #4, #5 to Wall Street, J, M, Z to Braod Street

The Skyscraper Museum traces the history of New York City's skycrapers and skyline. There are architectural models, drawings, maps, photos and more.

SNUG HARBOR CULTURAL CENTER (Staten Island)
1000 Richmond Terrace   Tel. (718) 448-2500
Admission: $2 for gallery
Hours: Wed-Sun 12:00-5:00
Staten Island Ferry then bus S40.

The Harbor was founded by Robert Richard Randall as a home for "aged, decrepid and worn-out sailors." The Harbor's trustees moved the institution to a new site on the North Carolina coast. Temple Israel of Staten Island conducted its initial services in the Sailor's Snug Harbor. It was organized in 1948 and was Staten Island's first Reform congregation.

SOUTH STREET SEAPORT MUSEUM (see STOP. 38)
16 Fulton Street   Tel. (212) 748-8600
Admission: $6 adults, $5 seniors, $4 students

Hours: Daily 10:00-6:00, Thur 10:00-8:00
Subway: #3, #4, #5, J, M, Z to Fulton Street

STATEN ISLAND BOTANICAL GARDEN (Staten Island)
1000 Richmond Terrace   Tel. (718) 273-8200
Admission: Free
Hours: Daily 8:00-sunset
Staten Island Ferry then bus S40.

The Staten Island Botanical Garden is located at the Snug Harbor Cultural Center.

STATEN ISLAND CHILDREN'S MUSEUM (Staten Island)
1000 Richmond Terrace   Tel. (718) 273-2060
Admission: $4
Hours: Tues-Sun 12:00-5:00 (only during the school year)
Staten Island Ferry then bus S40

STATEN ISLAND FERRY COLLECTION (Staten Island)
Located in the Ferry Terminal Waiting Room (St. George)
Tel. (718) 727-1135
Admission: $1
Hours: Daily 9:00-2:00

This is an exhibition of the history of the Staten Island Ferry with artifacts, historic postcards and photographs.

STATEN ISLAND INSTITUTE OF ARTS & SCIENCES (Staten Island)
75 Stuyvesant Place   Tel. (718) 727-1135
Admission: $2.50 adults, $1.50 seniors/students
Hours: Mon-Sat 9:00-5:00, Sun 1:00-5:00
Staten Island Ferry, then walk two blocks.

STATUE OF LIBERTY (See **STOP. 4**)
Liberty Island   Tel. (212) 363-3267
Ferry Information   Tel. (212) 269-5755
Admission: (Ferry) $7 adults, $3 children under 17
Hours: Daily 9:30-3:30
Ferry located in Castle Clinton - Battery Park
Subway: #1/9 to South Ferry, N or R to Whitehall Street

THE STUDIO MUSEUM IN HARLEM
144 West 125th Street   Tel. (212) 864-4500
Admission: $5 adults, $3 seniors/students
Hours: Wed-Fri 10:00-5:00, Sat-Sun 1:00-6:00
Subway: #2, #3, #4, #5, #6 to 125th Street

THE SWISS INSTITUTE
495 Broadway   Tel. (212) 925-2035
Admission: Free
Hours: Tues-Sat 11:00-6:00
Subway: N or R to Prince Street

TIBETAN MUSEUM (Staten Island)
338 Lighthouse Avenue   Tel. (718) 987-3500
Admission: $3 adults, $1 seniors/students
Hours: Wed-Sun 1:00-5:00

The Jacques Marchais Museum of Tibetan Art is a unique museum of Asian art with gardens. The buildings resemble a mountain temple with peaceful atmosphere.

UKRAINIAN MUSEUM
203 Second Avenue   Tel. (212) 228-0110
Admission: $1 adults, $ .50 seniors/students
Hours: Wed-Sun 1:00-5:00
Subway: L to Third Avenue

The collection includes 19th and 20th century Ukrainian folk art and splendid examples of some of its most colorful forms: Easter egg paintin and embroidery.

UNITED NATIONS HEADQUARTERS (See STOP. 140)
First Avenue & 46th Street   Tel. (212) 963-4440

VALENTINE-VARIAN HOUSE (The Bronx)
Bainbridge Avenue & 208th Street   Tel. (718) 881-8900
Admission: $2
Hours: Sat 10:00-4:00, Sun 1:00-5:00
Subway: D to 205th Street

This fieldstone farmhouse built in 1775 was moved from its original location across the street on Van Cortlandt Avenue East in the 1960s. The building is today home of the Bronx County Historical Society and the site of a museum of local history: photos, postcards, old beer bottles, arrowheads and cartridges and topical exhibits.

VAN CORTLANDT HOUSE MUSEUM (The Bronx)
Broadway & West 246th Street   Tel. (718) 543-3344
Hours: Tues-Fri 10:00-3:00, Sat-Sun 11:00-4:00
Subway: #1/9 to 242nd Street

The Van Cortlandt House was built as a mansion in 1748 and features 17th and 18th century Dutch, English and American furnishings.

VISUAL ARTS MUSEUM
209 East 23rd Street   Tel. (212) 592-2144
Admission: Free
Hours: Mon-Thur 9:00-8:00, Fri 9:00-5:00
Subway: #6 to 23rd Street

WAVE HILL CENTER FOR THE PERFORMING ARTS (The Bronx)
Independence Avenue & West 249th Street   Tel. (718) 549-3200
Admission: $4 adults, $2 seniors/students
Hours: Tues-Sun 9:00-5:30, Sat 9:00-12:00
Subway: #1/9 to 242nd Street

Wave Hill is a 28-acre estate, garden and cultural center overlooking the Hudson River. It was given to the city by financier George W. Perkins. Arturo Toscanini, Theodore Roosevelt and Mark Twain each lived here for a short time. The 19th century mansion hosts a chamber music series.

WHITNEY MUSEUM OF AMERICAN ART
Madison Avenue & 75th Street   Tel. (212) 570-3676
Admission: $8 adults, $6 seiors/students (Free on Thur evening)
Hours: Wed 11:00-6:00, Thur 1:00-8:00, Fri-Sun 11:00-6:00
Subway: #6 to 77th Street

WHITNEY MUSEUM AT PHILIP MORRIS
120 Park Avenue   Tel. (212) 878-2550
Admission: Free
Hours: Mon-Fri 11:00-6:00
Subway: #4, #5, #6, #7 to Grand Central

WORLD FINANCIAL CENTER (Winter Garden) (See **STOP. 34**)
West & Liberty Streets   Tel. (212) 945-0505

WORLD TRADE CENTER (Observation Deck) (See **STOP. 33**)
2 World Trade Center   Tel. (212) 323-2340
Admission: $12 adults, $9 seniors, $6 children
Hours: Daily 9:30-9:30 (summer 9:30-11:30)

YESHIVA UNIVERSITY MUSEUM (See **STOP. 123**)
2520 Amsterdam Avenue (185th Street) Tel. (212) 960-5390
Admission: $3 adults, $2 seniors/students
Hours: Tues-Thur 10:30-5:00, Sun 12:00-6:00
Subway: #1/9 to 181st Street

Eating

Kosher

Publisher's Note...

Although every effort has been made to ensure accuracy, changes will occur after this guide has gone to press.

Particular attention must be drawn to the fact that kosher food establishments change hands often and suddenly, in some cases going over to a non-kosher owner.

No responsiblity, therefore, can be taken for the absolute accuracy of the information, and travelers are advised to obtain confirmation of kashruth claims.

Restaurants and delis which are open for regular business on the Sabbath are *not* listed in this guide (even though some may have acquired kashruth certificates for their food products from local rabbis).

Let's Find a Kosher Restaurant

MEAT

Abigail's (Kof-K)   9 East 37th Street (Fifth Avenue)   Tel. (212) 725-0130
Alexi 56 (OU) (French)   25 West 56th St (Fifth Avenue)   Tel. (212) 767-1234
Blue Moon (OK Labs) (Japanese) 325 Fifth Ave (32nd St)   Tel. (212) 213-1110
Cafe Classico (Kof-K & OK Labs) (Italian)   35 West 57th St   Tel. (212) 3555411

Chick Chack Chicken   121 University Place   Tel. (212) 228-3100
China Shalom II (Kof-K)   686 Columbus Avenue (93 St)   Tel. (212) 662-9676
Colbeh (Kof-K) (Persian)   43 West 39th Street   Tel. (212) 354-8181
Deli Glatt (Vaad of Flatbush)   150 Fulton Street   Tel. (212) 349-3622

Deli Kasbah (Kof-K)   251 West 85th Street   Tel. (212) 496-1500
Domani Ristorante (Italian) (OK)   1590 First Avenue (82nd St)   Tel. 717-7575
Dougie's (Kof-K)   20 John Street   Tel. (212) 693-2422
         222 West 72nd Street   Tel. (212) 724-2222

Esthihana Oriental (Kof-K)   221 West 79th Street   Tel. (212) 501-0393
Galil (Kof-K)   1252 Lexington Avenue (85 St) Tel. (212) 439-9886
Gan-Asia (Thai-Chinese) (Vaad of Flatbush) 691 Amsterdam Ave   Tel. 280-3800
Glatt Dynasty (Kof-K) (Chinese)   1049 Second Avenue (55 St)   Tel. 888-9119

Gotham Grill (Kof-K)   127 West 72nd Street   Tel. (212) 787-8700
The Grand Deli (OU) (Chinese)   399 Grand Street   Tel. (212) 477-5200
Ha'ikara (OU) (Japanese)   1016 Second Avenue (53 St)   Tel. (212) 355-7000
Jasmine (Persian)   11 East 30th Street   Tel. (212) 251-8884

Jerusalem Pita   212 East 45th Street (Second Ave) Tel. (212) 922-0009
Ken & David Deli   249 East 45th Street   Tel. (212) 986-4704
Kosher Delight (Vaad of Flatbush) 1365 Broadway (37 St) Tel. (212) 563-3366
       1156 Sixth Avenue (45 St)   Tel. (212) 869-6699

The Kosher Tea Room (OK Labs) (Italian) 193 Second Ave Tel. (212) 677-2947
Le Marais (OK Labs) (French)   150 West 46th Street   Tel. (212) 869-0900
Levana's (Kof-K)   141 West 69th Street (Broadway)   Tel. (212) 877-8457
Mendy's Steak House (OK Labs)   61 East 34th Street   Tel. (212) 576-1010

Mendy's West Sports Club (OK Labs)   208 West 70th Street Tel. 877-6787
Mr. Broadway (OU) (Chinese)   1372 Broadway (37 St) Tel. (212) 921-2152
Pita Express   261 First Avenue (15th Street)   Tel. (212) 533-1956
      1470 Second Avenue (77th St)   Tel. (212) 674-1502

Polanco (Mexican) (OK) 502 Amsterdam Avenue (84th St)   Tel. (212) 799-1434
Tevere 84 (OU) (Italian)   155 East 84th Street (Lex. Ave) Tel. (212) 744-0210
Village Crown (Kof-K)   96 Third Avenue (12th Street)   Tel. (212) 674-2061

DAIRY

All American Health Cafe (OK Labs)   24 East 42nd Street Tel. 370-4525
American Cafe & Health Bar (Kof-K)   160 Broadway Tel. (212) 732-1426
La Bagel   263 First Avenue (16th Street) Tel. (212) 338-9292
Bissele (OK Labs)   127 West 72nd Street Tel. (212) 724-0377
                         1435 Second Avenue (75th Street) Tel. (212) 717-2333

Boychik's   19 West 45th St. Tel. (212) 719-5999
Cafe 1-2-3 (MBK)   2 Park Avenue (32nd St) Tel. (212) 685-7117
Cafe 18 (Kof-K)   8 East 18th Street Tel. (212) 620-4182
Cafe Roma Pizza (Kof-K)   Amsterdam Ave & 91st Street Tel. (212) 875-8972

Cafe Tal (Breuers)   11 West 47th Street Tel. (212) 575-3825
Diamond Dairy (CRC)   4 West 47th Street Tel. (212) 719-2694
Gertel's Bake Shop (CRC)   53 Hester Street Tel. (212) 982-3250
Great American Health Bar (OK Labs)   49 Ann Street Tel. (212) 587-8101

Jerusalem II (OU)   1375 Broadway (38th Street) Tel. (212) 819-1475
The Jewish Museum Cafe (STAR-K)   Fifth Avenue & 92nd St. Tel. 423-3200
Joseph's Cafe (MBK)   50 West 72nd Street Tel. (212) 595-5004
Kosher Dairy Restaurant   223 West 19th Street Tel. (212) 645-9315

Le Petit Cafe   96 Orchard Street   Tel. (2120 473-5488
Mizrachi Kosher Pizza (CKU)   105 Chambers Street   Tel. (212) 964-2280
Mom's Bagels (Kof-K)   15 West 45th Street   Tel. (212) 764-1566
my most favorite dessert company (OU)   120 W. 45th St. Tel. (212) 997-5130

Pizza Cave (OU)   218 West 72nd Street Tel. (212) 874-3700
Provi Provi (OK Labs) (Italian) 228 West 72nd Street Tel. (212) 875-9020
Ratner's (Kof-K)   138 Delancey Street   Tel. (212) 677-5588
Royale Bake Shop & Cafe (Breuers)   237 West 72nd Street Tel. 874-5642

Vegetarian Garden (Kof-K) (Italian)   15 East 40th Street Tel. (212) 545-7444
Village Crown (Kof-K) (Italian)   93 Third Avenue Tel. (212) 777-8816
Va Bene (OU) (Italian)   1589 Second Avenue (83rd St.) Tel. (212) 517-4448

VEGETARIAN

Caravan of Dreams   405 East 6th Street (First Avenue) Tel. (212) 254-1613
Madras Mahal (Indian)   104 Lexington Avenue (27th St) Tel. (212) 684-4010
Pongal (Indian)   110 Lexington Avenue Tel. (212) 696-9458
Tashi Awen (Chinese) 210 West 14th Street (Seventh Ave) Tel. (212)633-8823

Where
to
Pray

Where to Find a Synagogue

ORTHODOX

Cong. Talmud Torah Adereth El	135 East 29th Street	Tel. (212) 685-0241
Congregation Beth Israel	347 West 34th Street	Tel. (212) 279-0016
Beth Israel Center	264 West 91st Street	Tel. (212) 874-6135
Bialystoker Synagogue	7 Willett Street	Tel. (212) 475-0165
Congregation B'nai Israel Chaim	353 West 84th Street	Tel. (212) 874-0644
Carlebach Shul	305 West 79th Street	Tel. (212) 580-2391
Civic Center Synagogue	49 White Street	Tel. (212) 966-7141
Community Synagogue Center	325 East 6th Street	Tel. (212) 473-3665
Congregation Derech Amuno	53 Charles Street	Tel. (212) 242-6425
Congregation Emunath Israel	236 West 23rd Street	Tel. (212) 675-2819
Fifth Avenue Synagogue	5 East 62nd Street	Tel. (212) 838-2122
First Roumanian-American Cong.	89 Rivington Street	Tel. (212) 673-2835
Fur Center Synagogue	230 West 29th Street	Tel. (212) 594-9480
Garment Center Congregation	205 West 40th Street	Tel. (212) 391-6966
The Jewish Center	131 West 86th Street	Tel. (212) 724-2700
Congregation Kehilath Jeshurun	125 East 85th Street	Tel. (212) 427-1000
Lincoln Square Synagogue	200 Amsterdam Avenue	Tel. (212) 874-6100
Lisker Congregation	163 East 69th Street	Tel. (212) 472-3968
Millinery Center Synagogue	1025 Sixth Avenue	Tel .(212) 921-1580
Congregation Ohab Zedek	118 West 95th Street	Tel. (212) 749-5150
Congregation Ohav Sholom	270 West 84th Street	Tel. (212) 877-5850
Congregation Orach Chaim	1459 Lexington Avenue	Tel. (212) 722-6566
Park East Synagogue	163 East 67th Street	Tel. (212) 737-6900
Congregation Ramath Orah	550 West 110th Street	Tel. (212) 222-2470
Congregation Shearith Israel	8 West 70th Street	Tel. (212) 873-0300
Wall Street Synagogue	47 Beekman Street	Tel. (212) 227-7800
West Side Institutional Synagogue	122 West 76th Street	Tel. (212) 877-7652
Yorkville Synagogue	352 East 78th Street	Tel. (212) 249-0766
Young Israel of Fifth Avenue	3 West 16th Street	Tel. (212) 929-1525
Young Israel of Manhattan	225 East Broadway	Tel. (212) 732-0966
Young Israel of the West Side	210 West 91st Street	Tel. (212) 787-7513

CONSERVATIVE

Ansche Chesed Congregation	251 West 100th Street	Tel. (212) 865-9588
Congregation B'nai Jeshurun	270 West 89th Street	Tel. (212) 787-7600
Brotherhood Synagogue	28 Gramercy Park South	Tel. (212) 674-5750
Conservative Synagogue of Fifth Avenue	11 East 11th Street	Tel. 929-6954

East 55th Street Conservative Synagogue	308 E. 55th St.	Tel. (212) 752-1200
Cong. Ezrath Israel (Actors' Temple)	339 West 47th Street	Tel. (212) 245-6975
Congregation Habonim	44 West 66th Street	Tel. (212) 787-5347
Park Avenue Synagogue	50 East 87th Street	Tel. (212) 369-2600

Congregation Shaare Zedek	212 West 93rd Street	Tel. (212) 874-7005
Sutton Place Synagogue	225 East 51st Street	Tel. (212) 593-3300
Town & Village Temple	334 East 14th Street	Tel. (212) 677-8090

REFORM

Congregation Beth Simchat Torah	57 Bethune Street	Tel. (212) 929-9498
Central Synagogue	123 East 55th Street	Tel. (212) 838-5122
East End Temple	398 Second Avenue	Tel. (212) 254-8518
Temple Emanu-El	1 East 65th Street	Tel. (212) 744-1400

Temple Israel of the City of New York	112 East 75th Street	Tel. 249-5000
Metropolitan Synagogue of New York	10 Park Avenue	Tel. (212) 679-8580
Congregation Rodef Sholom	7 West 83rd Street	Tel. (212) 362-8800
Temple Shaaray Tefila	250 East 79th Street	Tel. (212) 535-7597

Stephen Wise Free Synagogue	30 West 68th Street	Tel. (212) 877-4050
Village Temple	33 East 12th Street	Tel. (212) 674-2340

RECONSTRUCTIONIST

Society for the Advancement of Judaism	15 West 86 St.	Tel. (212) 724-7000
Village Havurah	70 East 10th Street #168	Tel. (212) 485-7831

NOTE: The Resource Line of the UJA-Federation of New York offers free and confidential information about services relating to Jewish culture, synagogues, singles activities, employment, vocational training, housing, teen programs, Jewish education, the elderly, hospitals and family counseling.
Call (212) 753-2288

Biography

Oscar Israelowitz was born in Brussels, Belgium. He has degrees in architecture and geology and has traveled extensively throughout Europe, the United States, Canada, Africa and Israel. He is an architectural consultant by profession and is registered in the Register of Engineers and Architects in Israel.

Some of his architectural projects include the *Synagogue and Holocaust Center* of the Bobover chassidim and the *Yeshiva Rabbi Chaim Berlin*, both in Brooklyn, NY. He has also designed homes and villas for clients in the United States, Haiti and Israel.

Mr. Israelowitz is a professional photographer. His works have been on exhibit at the Whitney Museum of American Art in a show called *Watch the Closing Doors - Mosaics of the New York City Subways* (1973). That exhibit traveled to the Brooklyn Museum and has been incorporated into a permanent exhibition at the New York City Transit Museum. *The Changing Face of New York's Synagogues* was on exhibit at the Yeshiva University Museum in 1976. *Brooklyn: The City of Churches and Synagogues* was on display at Saint Joseph's College Gallery in Brooklyn in 1979 and traveled to the Long Island (now Brooklyn) Historical Society and to the Main Branch of the Brooklyn Public Library at Grand Army Plaza. In all of these exhibitions Mr. Israelowitz served as the guest curator and project coordinator.

Oscar Israelowitz has appeared on several television and radio programs including the *Joe Franklin Show*, NBC's *First Estate - Religion in Review*, and the Ruth Jacobs' *Jewish Home Show*.

In more recent years, Mr. Israelowitz has been conducting tours of the Lower East Side, Ellis Island and chassidic neighborhoods in Brooklyn. These tours have been written-up in *New York Magazine*, the *Washington Post*, the *New York Times*, the *Los Angeles Times*, the *Chicago Tribune* and *Crain's New York Business*.

CATALOG

BROOKLYN - THE CENTENNIAL EDITION
by Brian Merlis 132 pages
ISBN 1-878741-33-0 **$19.95** (plus $2.50 shipping)

WELCOME BACK TO BROOKLYN
by Brian Merlis & Oscar Israelowitz
172 pages   ISBN 1-878741-14-4 **$19.95** (plus $2.50 shipping)

BROOKLYN - THE WAY IT WAS
by Brian Merlis 250 pages
(paper) ISBN 1-878741-20-9 **$24.95** (plus $2.50 shipping)
(hard cover) ISBN 1-878741-21-7 **$39.95** (plus $3.50 shipping)

BROOKLYN'S GOLD COAST - The Sheepshead Bay Communities
by Brian Merlis 160 pages
(paper) ISBN 1-878741-49-7 **$19.95** (plus $2.50 shipping)
(hard cover) ISBN 1-878741-48-9 **$24.95** (plus $3.00 shipping)

BOROUGH PARK CENTENNIAL EDITION
by Oscar Israelowitz 96 pages
ISBN 1-878741-36-5 **$19.95** (plus $2.50 shipping)

ELLIS ISLAND GUIDE with Lower Manhattan (1998 Edition)
by Oscar Israelowitz 128 pages
ISBN 1-878741-01-2 **$7.95** (plus $2.00 shipping)

JEWISH HERITAGE TRAIL OF NEW YORK
by Oscar Israelowitz 196 pages
ISBN 1-878741-37-3 **$14.95** (plus $2.00 shipping)

LOWER EAST SIDE TOURBOOK (6th Edition)
by Oscar Israelowitz 150 pages
ISBN 1-878741-38-1 **$9.95** (plus $2.00 shipping)

U.S. HOLOCAUST MEMORIAL MUSEUM
& WASHINGTON, D.C. GUIDE
by Oscar Israelowitz 126 pages
ISBN 1-878741-16-0 **$7.95** (plus $2.00 shipping)

NEW YORK CITY SUBWAY GUIDE
by Oscar Israelowitz 260 pages
ISBN 0-961103607-1 **$6.95** (plus $2.50 shipping)

EAT YOUR WAY THROUGH AMERICA
- A Kosher Dining Guide (4th Edition)
by Oscar Israelowitz   125 pages
ISBN 1-878741-32-2 **$6.95** (plus $1.75 shipping)

UNITED STATES JEWISH TRAVEL GUIDE (4th Edition)
by Oscar Israelowitz 460 pages
ISBN 1-878741-31-4 **$19.95** (plus $3.00 shipping)

GUIDE TO THE JEWISH WEST
by Oscar Israelowitz   320 pages
ISBN 1-878741-06-3 **$11.95** (plus $2.00 shipping)

EAT YOUR WAY THROUGH NEW YORK
by Oscar Israelowitz 125 pages
ISBN 1-878741-34-9 **$9.95** (plus $2.00 shipping)

GUIDE TO JEWISH EUROPE - Western Europe 9th Edition
by Oscar Israelowitz   354 pages
ISBN 1-878741-19-5 **$14.95** (plus $2.50 shipping)

ITALY JEWISH TRAVEL GUIDE
by Annie Sacerdoti   242 pages
ISBN 1-878741-15-2 **$14.95** (plus $2.50 shipping)

ISRAEL TRAVEL GUIDE
by Oscar Israelowitz   350 pages
ISBN 1-878741-26-8 **$19.95** (plus $2.50 shipping)

CANADA JEWISH TRAVEL GUIDE
by Oscar Israelowitz   196 pages
ISBN 1-878741-10-1 **$9.95** (plus $2.00 shipping)

SYNAGOGUES OF THE UNITED STATES
by Oscar Israelowitz   200 pages
 (paper) ISBN 1-878741-09-8 **$24.95** (plus $2.50 shipping)
 (hard cover) ISBN 1-878741-11-X **$29.95** (plus $3.00 shipping)

ISRAELOWITZ PUBLISHING
P.O.BOX 228 BROOKLYN, NY 11229
TEL. (718) 951-7072

TOURS OF JEWISH NEW YORK

LOWER EAST SIDE

This two-hour walking tour includes stops at the old Jewish Daily Forward Building, Seward Park's *Chazir Mark*, the Educational Alliance with its Hall of Fame and Chaim Gross Gallery, Shteeble Row, the Jewish Mural at the Bialystoker Home for the Aged, the last boys' yeshiva in the neighborhood, the Eldridge Street Synagogue, Orchard Street and, of course, Guss' Pickles with its outdoor pickle barrels.

JEWISH HERITAGE TRAIL

This two-hour walking tour includes stops at the Jewish Plymouth Rock, Fraunces Tavern, site of North America's first synagogue, Federal Hall - where George Washington was inaugurated first President of the United States, the New York Stock Exchange, Bowling Green, the Federal Reserve Bank - where Nazi gold was stored, Castle Clinton, Emma Lazarus' historic plaque, the Jerusalem Grove and the new Museum of Jewish Heritage - A Living Memorial to the Holocaust.

Note: Tour does not include entrance to the Museum of Jewish Heritage.

ELLIS ISLAND

This three-hour tour includes a ferry ride past the Statue of Liberty and a walking tour on Ellis Island with its Museum of Immigration and Wall of Honor, with over 400,000 names. The tour includes a visit to the archaeological remains of Fort Gibson, an exciting film about how the 12 million immigrants arrived and were processed, and a stop in the Great Hall with its magnificent Guastavino vaulted ceiling and beautiful chandeliers.

CHASSIDIC NEIGHBORHOODS OF BROOKLYN

This four-hour bus and walking tour includes visits to the Satmar Chassidim in Williamsburg, the Bobover Chassidim in Borough Park and the Lubavitcher Chassidim in Crown Heights. See the great synagogues established by each group. Depending on the time of year when visiting, see the hundreds of *succahs* built on specially-designed terraces, visit a matzoh factory and watch matzohs being created within the prescribed 18 minutes, and visit a mikveh and the Lubavichter Museum.

SYNAGOGUES OF NEW YORK

This four-hour bus tour includes visits to some of the prominant congregations in the city such as the Spanish and Portuguese Synagogue, Temple Emanu-El, the Central Synagogue, B'nai Jeshurun, the Bialystoker Synagogue, the Civic Center Synagogue - which seems to float between two century-old loft buildings, and Congregation Habonim - founded by Holocaust survivors and includes stone fragments of synagogues burned on Kristallnacht.
Note: Some congregations allow visits only on Sundays while others only allow visits on weekdays. Three or four synagogues would be included in each tour.

NOTE: These tours are designed for groups of ten or more.

ISRAELOWITZ TOURS

P.O.Box 228 Brooklyn, NY 11229
Tel. (718) 951-7072

Index

Abigail Adams Smith
        Museum, 133
Actor's Temple, 103
Aleichem, Sholom, 60
Alice Austen House, 133
Alternative Museum, 133
Altman, B., 60
American Craft Museum, 133
Amalgamated Dwellings, 56
American Indian Museum, 15
American Jewish
        Historical Society, 100
American Museum of the
        Moving Image, 133
American Museum of
        Natural History, 111, 134
American Numismatic Society, 134
Americas Society Art Gallery, 134
Anshe Slonim, 84
Anthology Film Archives, 134
Ararat Colony, 102
Archaeological Dig, 23
Arnold Toynbee Hall, 56
Aquarium, 8, 134
Arbiter Ring, 61
Asia Society Galleries, 135
Astor Library, 95
Audobon, John, J., 109
Leo Baeck Institute, 100
Baltimore, 8
Bank of the United States, 77
Bankruptcy Court, 15
Bard Graduate Center for
        Decorative Arts, 135
Barnum, P.T., 7
The Barry Sisters, 92
Bartholdi, F., 10
Bartow-Pell Mansion, 136
Beame, Mayor Abraham., 13
Bedloes Island, 7
Belmont, August, 14
Berger, W., 40
Berlin, 106
Herbert & Eileen Bernard
        Museum, 121
Bernstein, Leonard, 103

Beth Hamedrash Hagadol, 70
Beth Israel Hospital, 130
Bialystoker Home, 58
Bialystoker Synagogue, 71
Bintel Brief, 61
Black Fashion Museum, 135
Blatas, Arbit, 117
B'nai B'rith, 70
B'nai Jeshurun, 102, 111
Bonus, Ben, 92
Boss Tweed, 39, 54
Boston, 8
Breukelen, 24
The Bronx Museum
        of the Arts, 135
The Bronx Zoo, 136
Brooklyn Botanical Garden, 136
Brooklyn, Bridge, 40
Brooklyn Children's Museum, 136
Brooklyn Historical Society, 136
Brooklyn Museum of Art, 137
Bowling Green, 15
Budapest, 118
Cahan, Abraham, 61
Cairo Geniza, 114
Canal Street Theater, 66
Cantor, Eddie, 50, 60
Carnegie Hall, 103, 137
Castle Clinton, 7, 137
Castle Garden, 7
Castle Williams, 7
Cemeteries, 25, 40, 100
Center for Book Arts, 137
Center For Jewish History, 96
Central Park Zoo, 137
Central Railroad of NJ, 12
Central Synagogue, 118
Chagall, Marc, 103, 117
Chaim Gross Studio
        Museum, 137
Charging Bull, 15
Chasam Sopher, 82
Chazir Mark, 63
Children's Museum
        of Manhattan, 138

Children's Museum
of the Arts, 138
China Institute of America, 138
Church of St. Mary, 71
City Hall, 27, 37, 138
Clinton, DeWitt, 7
The Cloisters, 138
Commodities Exchange
Center, 138
Community Synagogue, 89
Conference House, 139
Cooper-Hewett Museum, 139
Le Corbusier, 114
Dahesh Museum, 139
de Lancey, Stephan, 22
DIA Center for the Arts, 139
DiModica, Arturo, 15
The Drawing Center, 140
Dutch-Indian Deal, 14
Dutch West India Company, 92
Dyckman House, 140
East Side Hebrew Institute, 91
East Side Torah Center, 56
East Side Mikveh, 56
Educational Alliance, 58
Eifel, G., 10
Eighth Street Shul, 89
Eldridge Street Synagogue,
48, 140
Ellis Island, 7, 10, 140
Empire State Building, 140
The Equitable Gallery, 141
Essex Street Market, 81
Federal Hall, 27, 141
Federal Reserve Bank, 32, 141
Feinstein, Rabbi Moshe, 64
Fernbach, Henry, 118
Floating Synagogue, 40
Folksbeine Yiddish Theater, 118
Forbes Magazine Galleries, 141
Fort Gibson, 7
Fort New Amsterdam, 16
Fort Wood, 7
Forverts, 61
Franks, Jacob, 25
Franks, Phila, 22
Fraunces Tavern, 21, 22, 141
Frick Collection, 141
Galveston, 8
Garden Cafeteria, 63
Garment Center Monument, 102

Gershwin, Ira, 68
Gilbert, Cass, 37
Gomez, Lewis, 25
Abraham Goodman House, 106
Governors Island, 7
Gracie Mansion, 142
Grand Canal, 20
Grant's Tomb, 142
Greek Jewish Museum, 75, 142
Greene, Lorne, 71
Grey Art Gallery, 142
Grimes, Tammy, 71
Gross, Chaim, 60, 137
Guastavino Tiles, 39
Guggenheim Museum, 142
Guiness World Records
Exhibit Hall, 143
Habonim Congregation, 106
Hall of Fame, 143
Hamilton, Alexander, 30
Hamilton Grange, 143
Harbor Defense Museum, 143
Hart, Ephraim, 27
Hayden Planetarium, 144
Hispanic Society of America, 144
Hebrew Arts School, 106
Hebrew Technical School, 92
Hebrew Union College, 95
Heins & LaFarge, 14
Henry Street Settlement, 54, 71
Heren Gracht, 20
Herter Brothers, 48, 64
HIAS, 95
Holocaust Memorials,
16, 106, 114, 117
Hudson River School, 109
Hunt, Morris, 30, 103
ILGWU, 58
Immigrants' Monument, 8
IRT, 14
Isaiah Wall, 117
International Center
of Photography, 144
Intrepid Sea-Air-Space
Museum, 144
Isamu Noguchi Garden
Museum, 144
Janina Synagogue, 75
Japan Society, 145
Jarmulowsky Bank, 66
Jay, John, 21

Jerusalem Grove, 13
Jewish Daily Forward, 61
Jewish Mural, 58
The Jewish Museum, 128, 145
Jewish Plymouth Rock, 20
Jewish Tenements, 64
Jewish Theological
    Seminary, 114, 145
Jews Hospital, 130
Judaica Museum, 145
Keaton, Diane, 71
Kennedy, Captain A., 16
Kessel Garden, 8
King George III, 15
Kletzker Brotherly Aid, 66
Kolleck, Teddy, 13
Kosher Winery, 82
Kousevitzky, Moshe, 79
Lazarus, Emma, 8
Leo Baeck Institute, 145
Levy, Asser, 24
Liberation Monument, 13
Liberty Science Center, 12
Liberty State Park, 12
Library & Museum
    of the Performing Arts, 145
Lincoln Center, 103, 146
Lind, Jenny, 7
Lovelace Tavern, 23
Lower East Side
    Tenement Museum, 73, 146
Lubavitcher Rebbe Museum, 146
de Lucena, A., 24
Ludlow Street Prison, 70
Mangin, J.F., 37
Manhattan Railway Co., 50
Marshall, Louis, 60
Macy's, 35, 60, 102
Marsh, Reginald, 15
Matthau, Walter, 70
Matzoh Factory, 82
McBean, T., 37
McComb, J., 37
McKim, Mead & White, 39, 96
Melville, Herman, 19
Merchants House Museum, 146
Merkin Concert Hall, 106
Mesifta Tifereth Jerusalem, 63
Mesquita, B.B., 44
Metropolitan Museum of Art, 146
Metropolitan Opera House,
    103, 106, 147

Mikveh, 56
Mill Street Synagogue, 25, 109
Moby Dick, 19
Morris-Jumel Mansion, 147
Mostel, Zero, 70
Mother Seton, 20
Mt. Sinai Hospital, 130
MTJ, 63
The Municipal Art Society, 147
Municipal Building, 39
Murray, Arthur, 60
El Museo Del Bario, 147
Museum of African Art, 147
Museum of American
    Financial History, 147
Museum of American
    Folk Art, 147
Museum of American
    Illustration, 148
Museum of American Indian, 15
Museum of the
    American Piano, 148
Museum of Chinese
    in the Americas, 148
Museum of the
    City of New York, 148
The Museum at FIT, 147
Museum of Jewish Heritage,
    16, 149
Museum of Modern Art, 149
Museum of Television
    & Radio, 149
Napoleon, 7
National Academy
    of Design, 149
National Museum of the
    American Indian, 149
National Museum of
    Catholic Arts, 150
NBC Tours, 150
Neimeyer, Oscar, 114
New Colossus, 10
New Museum of
    Contemporary Art, 150
Newseum, 150
New York Academy
    of Medicine, 150
New York Aquarium, 8, 134
New York
    Botanical Garden, 150
New York City
    Fire Museum, 151

New York City
Police Museum, 151
New York Hall of Science, 151
New-York Historical Society,
109, 152
New York Public
Library, 117, 152
New York Stock
Exchange, 27, 152
NY Transit Museum, 14, 152
New York Unearthed, 19, 152
92nd Street YMHA, 127, 153
Noah, Mordecai Manuel, 102
North Wind Undersea
Museum, 153
No. 1 Broadway, 16
Olympia & York, 32
127 John Street, 33
Oysher, Moishe, 79
Pacheco, R., 25
Paine Weber art Gallery, 153
Joseph Papp's
Public Theater, 95
Park Avenue Synagogue, 127
Park East Synagogue, 124
Peck, Gregory, 71
Peerce, Jan, 79
Pelli, Cesar, 32
Picon, Molly, 92
Pierpont Morgan Library, 153
Pike Street Shul, 52
Edgar Allan Poe Cottage, 153
Prospect Park Zoo, 153
Public Baths, 79
Queens Botanical Garden, 154
Queens County Farm
Museum, 154
Queens Historical Society, 154
Queens Museum of Art, 154
Rabbi Jacob Joseph
Yeshiva, 53, 70
Radio City Music Hall, 154
Ramaz Upper School, 124
Rapaport, Nathan, 13
Red Square, 84
Richmondtown Restoration, 154
Ridley's Department Store, 68
Ritualarium, 56
RJJ, 53
Roebling, John A., 40
Roche, Kevin, 16

Theodore Roosevelt
Birthplace, 155
Rosenblatt, Yossel, 79
Roth, Emery, 19, 30, 33
Roumaniashe Shul, 79
Saeltzer, Alexander, 84, 95
St. Augustine's Church, 54
St. Barbara's Church, 44
St. Elizabeth Ann Seton, 20
St. Paul's Chapel, 35
St. Teresa's Church, 53
Sarnoff, David, 60
Schapiro's Kosher Winery, 82
Schechter, Solomon, 114
Schermerhorn Row, 35
Schiff, Jacob. H.,
54, 60, 118, 127
17 State Street, 19
Seixas, G.M., 44
Seward Park, 63
Seward Park High School, 70
Shearith Israel, 20, 25, 27,
44, 100, 109
Shoah, 16
Shteebl Row, 57
Sidney Hillman Houses, 56
Single's Shuls, 114
Sinsheimer's Cafe, 70
The Skyscraper Museum, 155
Smithsonian, 15, 139
Snug Harbor
Cultural Center, 155
South Street Seaport Museum,
19, 35,155
Spanish & Portuguese Syn.,
20, 25, 44, 100, 109
Spektor, Rabbi I.E., 44
Spielberg, Steven, 16
Stadt Huys, 24
Staten Island Botanical
Garden, 156
Staten Island Children's
Museum, 156
Staten Island Ferry
Collection, 156
Staten Island Institute
of Art & Sciences, 156
Statue of Liberty, 10, 156
Stern, Isaac, 103
Straus, Isador, 35, 60, 102
Straus, Nathan, 63

Streits Matzoh Factory, 82
Studio Museum in Harlem, 156
Stuyvesant, Peter, 92
Subway Kiosk, 14
Sunshine Theater, 84
Supreme Court, 21
Surrogate's Court, 39
Swiss Institute, 157
Synagogue Space, 88
Temple Emanu-El, 121
Tenement Museum, 73, 146
Tibetan Museum, 157
Tiffany, Louis Comfort, 109, 121
Titanic Memorial, 33, 60, 102
Tifereth Jerusalem, 63
Transit Museum, 14
Triangle Fire, 96
Tribeca, 40
Trinity Church, 28
Tucker, Richard, 79, 106
Twain, Mark, 60
Tweed Courthouse, 39
Ukrainian Museum, 157
Union Square, 58
Union Square Church, 78
United Nations Headquarters,
            114, 157
U.S. Bankruptcy Court, 15
U.S. Custom House, 14
United States Lines, 16
University Settlement House, 78
Upjohn, Richard, 30
Valentine-Varian House, 157
Van Cortlandt House
            Museum, 157

Vanderbilt, Mrs. Cornelius, 127
Vietnam Veterans Memorial, 25
Visual Arts Museum, 158
Wald, Lilian, 54
Wallach, Eli, 71
War of 1812, 7
Warburg, Felix, 60, 128
Washington Arch, 96
Washington, George, 16,
            22, 28, 37
Watson, James, 19
Wave Hill Center, 158
West Side Story, 103
Whitney Museum
            of American Art, 158
Williamsburg Bridge, 73
Wintergarden, 32
Woolworth Building, 37
Workmen's Circle, 61
WPA, 15
World Financial Center, 30, 158
World Trade Center, 30, 158
Yamasaki, Minoru, 30
Yellin, S., 33
Yeshiva University, 44,
Yeshiva University Museum,
            100, 158
Yiddish Theater District,
            91, 118
YIVO, 100, 148
York & Sawyer, 32